I'M MAD ~~AS~~ AT HELL

A JOURNEY TO SANCTIFIED, SATISFIED, AND SINGLE

UNDERSTANDING THE DYNAMICS OF SPIRITUAL WARFARE AND DOMESTIC VIOLENCE

Second Edition

Maxine Lloyd

ML Ministries
www.mlministries.org

Cover Design by KKProductions www.kkproductions.com
Wanda J. Banks, Editor
Maxine Lloyd, Revising Editor

Library of Congress Control Number: 2007938424

Published by ML Ministries
P. O. Box 612
Columbia, MD 21045
www.mlministries.org

Printed in the Unites States of America

ISBN-13: 978-0-9800226-0-5 (previously ISBN-13: 978-0-9761322-2-6)
ISBN-10: 0-9800226-0-6 (previously 10: 0-9761322-2-2)

TABLE OF CONTENTS

ACKNOWLEDGEMENTS

I am in awe of the wonderful works of God. I didn't understand it then, but I understand it now. God is our greatest cheerleader. After all, God says, " For I know the thoughts that I think toward you, saith the Lord, thoughts of peace, and not of evil, to give you an expected end" (Jeremiah 29:11). All glory and honor goes to God alone and the people God put in my way to bring me to this day. I thank my children, Rachita, Ranita, and Rajah; my diamonds in the rough. We have gone through many trials, disagreements, anger, and misunderstandings, but through it all, you have loved me sometimes in spite of me and in spite of your- selves. Your courage and tenacity to keep your faith and the love of God in your hearts is what encourages me each and everyday. Everyday I thank God that you have not given up, and I pray that in some way my courage to live and not die through all of the hurt has given you the strength and courage to live on. Your love, joy, peace, healing, and wholeness are the most important things in life to me. If I could make your life free of pain and suffering, I would, but, I am not God. God has you in the palm of His hand and no one can pluck you out. God knows your expected end, too. I thank God for Rev. Dr. Lee P. Washington, my pastor, who gave me the courage to remove myself from a dangerous and abusive relationship. His belief and acknowledgment of my pain opened the door for me to walk free from my abuser. That day was the first day of the rest of my life. May God bless you richly. To my professors at Howard University School of Divinity, Dr. Cheryl Sanders, Dr. Delores Carpenter, Dr. Bernard Richardson, Dr. Cameron Byrd, Dr. Michael Newheart, Bishop Joseph Taylor, Dr. Kwasi Kwakye-Nuako, Dr. Ronald Hopson, Dr. Kortright Davis and Dr. Alice Bellis, you stretched me and my faith. I grew up to the hard realities of life and discovered and experienced God in the midst. To Dr. Breeskin, Head of the Psychology Department at the University of Maryland, you helped me to understand the underlying factors of people experiencing Abnormal Psychosis and for showing me the importance of getting professional help from those trained to help move us from brokenness to wholeness.

To my Pastors, Reverends Henry and Renee Cole, words cannot explain, time does not allow nor can space in this book contain my heartfelt thanks and gratitude for breathing life back into me so that I could became a living soul again. I thank Brandon and Taylor for sharing their parents with me and my children. People may never understand our relationship, but we are family. The long days, the long nights, early morning phone calls, going out searching and bringing back my child, (she knows who I am talking about) the months, the years, the hospitals, in and out of court rooms, doctor's appointments, school visits, talks, prayers, through the tears, through the anger, misunderstandings, and understandings, we are still here. I thank you. I thank you. I thank you. You are true shepherd pastors that give all for their sheep. To God be the glory!

To Kendall King and KK Productions, you have made the project beautiful with your gift of art, thank you. To Angela Merchant, my beautician, your head massages and listening ear contributed to my healing. In case you didn't know, your healing hands gave me life and comfort each time I sat in your chair. A special thanks to Kevin and Karen Prue who believed in me enough to plant the first seeds of faith to help make this book a published blessing to the many families whose lives will be touched and changed.

It is easy when people are visibly cheering you on, encouraging you, and coaching you. Not only for the one being encouraged and coached, but also, it's a challenge to those who have to pray for you in silence and never let you know that they are praying for you. You know who you are. I thank God for your obedience. I thank my publisher, EoH Publishing, who made it possible for this book to make it to the world and become a best seller. I thank God for opening your heart to give me the opportunity to share with the world a journey from a shattered past to a God ordained and gloriously purposed filled life and

A Journey From As to At

Sanctified, Satisfied, & Single

Maxine shares her escape from a life of chaos and disorder to the arms of a loving God where she is secure from assault and violation (**sanctification**). She understood and lived her life from the perspective as someone who took on the character and condition of those living in a realm where the damned suffer everlasting punishment and where there was no hope of escape.

Maxine has put an end to all the doubts and uncertainty (**satisfied**) to make the truth known to everyone that we are all separate and unique and whole (**single**), no longer broken or deceived by the wiles of the devil. She has been liberated in Christ and has arrived at: Sanctified, Satisfied and Single.

FOREWORD

Maxine Lloyd through her book, <u>I'm Mad at Hell, A Journey to Sanctified, Satisfied, and Single</u> has heard by the hearing of her ears, and seen by the seeing of her eyes, and felt by the deepest feeling of her heart, the good news of God in a bad experience.

Domestic violence is one of those growing concerns that will so change your life until all you can do is call out to God. This book offers a personal account of pain and glory. Reading this work challenges you to embrace a refreshing, encouraging, enlightening, comforting and life transforming experience.

If you have come out of a painful, damaging, and traumatic past; if you have experienced empty, broken, or unfulfilled relationships; if you are tired of feeling unloved, disconnected, or lonely; then you will enjoy reading this book. Additionally, this book serves as a guide for interaction with God and your inner healing.

I salute Rev. Maxine for her timely expression and sharing understanding of God's Response at Chaotic Events (GRACE). There is much healing within these grace filled pages. Who among us doesn't need that?

Because He Lives I Am,
Rev. Dr. Lee P. Washington
Senior Pastor, Reid Temple AME Church

PREFACE

Theology has one problem, God (Jurgen Moltman)[1]. A living faith is one of the principal sources of theology. Living faith seeks to reason and understand that which is to be believed about God. Thus, the object of living faith is God, and only God can reveal who God is through self-disclosure. God is Spirit. God has never been seen, heard, nor touched. Yet, that which is believed is always being revealed, never ends, and continues to unfold until the future consummation of God is attained. God's self-disclosure to humanity is done in many ways. One way of God's self-disclosure is through Jesus Christ, which defines Christian faith. Christian living faith, therefore, uses religious language of "God talk" to describe and project a reality of that we do not know, but believe as if we know. Living faith expresses itself through religious language that helps to reflect and grasp understanding of who God is and the interactions which God has with humanity.

Expressions of living faith have been kept alive for thousands of years and have been passed on in the forms of one's culture, traditions, language, values, beliefs, and symbols. Traditions have been passed down through culture and socialized to human- kind at specific eras of time to help see the ever changing interpretations of who God is and that God truly exists. First, traditions were passed down orally then in written literary texts for our knowledge.

Literary writings are many and none can stand alone, however, in Christian faith, these writing have been codified into the bible, which is the norm for Christian belief. Next, creeds such as the Apostle's Creed have given a foundation to values and beliefs of Christian doctrine. Writings in religious language help to speak about ultimate truths, which cannot otherwise be expressed. Last, religious language helps to mediate experiences, produce access to inner life, and resurrect a bridge that connects people to God. Problems can arise in religious language when language differ and understanding is lost, and translation of symbols, metaphors, parables, and analogies are misinterpreted. Consequently, religious language can free or imprison people who may or may not have the same culture. In cultures where the language is the same and understood, religious language expressed in the community of faith is shared to help people connect to God and to one another.

Living faith for Christians is lived out in the context of the church. The church is where Christians learn to live out the important things in life, to teach others the ministry and purpose of the church, including pastoral and prophetic ministry; learn the proper interpretation of scriptures, and understand the historical and contextual interpretations of Christian methods as it unfolds in every age.

Living faith, as a principal source of theology, gives the foundation on which experiences can stand and what is believed about God. Living faith helps to affirm God is, even though it cannot be proved that God exists.

Faith calls forth theology. We believe and constantly seek to understand God. This belief is actively at work each day, trying to lay hold of the unrealities of hope by bringing them into the realm of realities through what is written, what is experienced, what is tradition, and what is intellectually understood.

What we believe leads us to articulate that which we believe to others who may believe differently from what we believe. In order to articulate what we believe, we defer to the language of faith that will help others to understand the infinite God and will bring God into the finite understanding of human existence.

We seek to understand and study God through that which is written including: scriptures, historical documents, anthropological findings, and other written texts from various theologians, and other religions. Also, we seek to understand and study God through that which God chooses to reveal to us through self –disclosure, through what we experience personally through revelatory events and testimonies of others and their experiences. Traditions passed down through our culture and socialized to us at specific eras of time, help us to see the ever changing interpretations of crises, conflicts, day-to-day living, and social norms. Finally, we seek understanding of our faith through that which is intellectually revealed through the sciences, our own personal pursuits, inquiry, and reflection.

Theology is ever changing because each individual's faith is an active motivating factor and energizing force that will allow one to be who they are and do what they do at any given point in time and space. If an assessment is made of the following scriptures,

Romans 5:1 *Therefore being justified by faith, we have peace with God through our Lord Jesus Christ:*

Ephesians 2:8 *For by grace are ye saved through faith; and that not of yourselves: it is the gift of God:*

Hebrew 11:1 *Now faith is the substance of things hoped for, the evidence of things not seen.*

as Christians, we will come to understand in whom and what we believe; namely, justification by faith, saving faith, and believing/knowing faith, respectively. The Christian faith represents- in religious language- the treatment of, "I believe" as the highest level of certainty. Therefore, faith is a distinct human action of which we exercise our strong trust to justify our actions and devotion to that of the God of Jesus.

Believing faith (as understood in Hebrews 11:1), says, "Faith is of things hoped for and a confidence in matters not seen, but yet with conviction it is belief, regardless of whether or not it is provable". It is by this faith that the Christian can participate in the promise of salvation. The belief is so overwhelming that it has the character of knowing, which is the highest level of certainty. Thus, as a Christian believer, we grasp and hold onto the belief that faith in Jesus Christ, the one who justified us and gave us redemption and salvation through his death, burial and resurrection, reconciles us back into a right relationship with God.

John Calvin in his article, "The Nature of Faith", sums it up as, "*a steady and certain knowledge of the divine benevolence towards us, which is founded upon the truth of the gracious promise of God in Christ, and is both revealed to our minds and sealed in our hearts by the Holy Spirit.*"[3] *Built upon this definition of faith, having been declared righteous, then, by faith, we have peace toward God through our Lord Jesus Christ (Romans 5:1 YLT) and by grace ye are having been saved, through faith, and this not of you -- of God the gift, (Ephesians 2:8 YLT).*

Martin Luther's doctrine of justification by faith alone made faith the cornerstone for believers to accept God's grace of salvation. God does everything necessary for salvation, thus the phrase, "justification by grace through faith" brings out the meaning of the doctrine more clearly: The justification (cleared of guilt or made in right relationship) of the sinner is based upon God's unmerited favor (grace) and is received through faith (believing).[4]

So how do we reconcile and recognize God in the midst of suffering, failure, and disappointment? In order to speak first of God, we must realize that we speak of God in God talk or language that has no empirical proof. However, we speak with moral certainty and compelling faith that the love of God is sovereign and God's justice is emphasized in the fact that *God draws near to us and God does not compromise, but is faithful to God's divine freedom and integrity.*[5]

For the Christian faith believers, we recognize God's presence in the midst of suffering, failure, and disappointment by the witness and experience of God with Israel, Jesus Christ, the church, and in our own personal lives. It is through our own moral integrity and notions that we are given to attributing divine meaning and character to God and God's dispensation of mercy, justice, kindness, goodness, holiness, righteousness, blessedness, truth, and love in the presence of human suffering, failure, and disappointment.

In the history of Israel; in the historical accounts of Jesus' life, death, and resurrection; in the history of the church after Jesus' ascension, and in our personal lives, we hear and experience a living God who is personally involved in the good times and bad times, sharing in suffering, in failure, in disappointment, in joy and celebration, and in faithfully manifesting God's presence of love and justice.

We speak of God's presence in failure and disappointment as universal, unconditional, initiating, faithful, and reconciling love. In the historical accounts of Israel, Jesus' life, the church and in our own personal lives, we find God's love for all people was made manifest in Jesus Christ. This love is offered to all in spite of our limitations, unfaithfulness, discriminations, and sin. God always acts first in our behalf to bring us back to a personal relationship with God and with one another. This is attested in scripture: Jacob and Esau (anger), Amnon and Tamar (rape), Abigail and Nabal (emotional abuse), Lot and his daughters (incest), and Absalom and Amnon (fratricide).

In suffering, God loved us so much, that he did not leave us alone, but took upon God's self the form of man and came to live and dwell with us. God with us-- Immanuel, in the man Jesus Christ, clearly sees the differences in God's people; the rich and poor, the powerful and the powerless, the privileged and underprivileged, those who are defenseless, the oppressors and the oppressed. It is with those who suffer, are weak, excluded, and downtrodden that God's loving justice prevails. Not in giving people what they deserve, but in giving them what they need. The witness of *God's suffering love is with the Old Testament prophets and in the New Testament with Jesus' compassion with the sick, His solidarity with the poor, and His passion and resurrection.*[6]

God's unchangeable, immutable, and immovable attributes assures us that God is constant, consistent, dependable, and faithful in our relationship with God. God will meet us where we are. God is eternal (not limited by time), Omniscient (knows all things), and Omnipotent (there is nothing that God cannot do). God's omni-presence (no place where God is not) assures us that God is El Roi, the One who sees the injustices that occur in our lives and is always watching over us (provident). God also loves those whose lives are not according to God's love and good. Additionally, God's justice (100% fair in His actions with us) means that God is for and not against sinful people, but rather accepts and seeks to restore them to right relationships.[7] God's love is unconditional (agape) and beyond human comprehension (Matthew 5:45). God's attributes never get out of balance with each other, and God never acts out of character.[8]

We read and hear the historical accounts of God's presence in the life of Israel and the life of Jesus Christ during their time of failure, suffering, and disappointment. We too can only recognize the presence of God in our own failures, suffering, and disappointments as we seek to experience a relationship with God and God's creation that are filled with different people of other nations, cultures, races and gender. Through us, the moral attributes of mercy, justice, kindness, goodness, holiness, righteousness, blessedness, truth, and love that we have attributed to God must be made manifest in our own lives, so that others can experience God's presence in their time of failure, suffering and disappointment.

Notes

1 Faith Seeking Understanding, pp. 1-5

2 Hodgson, pg. 19

3 Christian Theology Reader, pp. 26

4 Christian Theology, An Introduction, pp.456-457

5 Christian Doctrine, pp. 104

6 Faith Seeking Understanding, pp. 71

7 Christian Doctrine, pp. 108

8 Strongman's His Name... What's His Game, pp. 1-2

FIRST THINGS FIRST

This book is written to all who believe or are willing to believe in the power of God and the finished work of Jesus Christ who died on the cross for your sins that you may live a life reconciled to God. Our first priority is to understand the "Great Commandment."

Jesus said unto him, thou shalt love the Lord thy God with all thy heart, and with all thy soul, and with all thy mind, this is the first and great commandment. And the second is like unto it, thou shalt love thy neighbor as thyself (Matthew 22:37-39).

If you have not confessed Jesus Christ as your Lord and Savior, asked him to forgive you of your sins, and to come live within your heart, you can do so now as easy as saying your ABC's. The bible says, "*but the natural man receiveth not the things of the Spirit of God: for they are foolishness unto him; neither can he know them, because they are spiritually discerned (1 Corinthians 2:14).*

You must first establish a relationship with God through God's son, Jesus Christ, to be able to understand the things discussed in this book. If you have confessed Christ as your Lord and Savior, be prayerful as you read this book and allow the Holy Spirit to speak to you and to minister to you about the deep spiritual things of God.

"Likewise the Spirit also helpeth our infirmities: for we know not what we should pray for as we ought: but the Spirit itself maketh intercession for us with groanings which cannot be uttered. And he that searcheth the hearts knoweth what is the mind of the Spirit, because he maketh intercession for the saints according to the will of God" (Romans 8:26-27).

If you would like to pray the prayer of salvation now, you can follow the simple ABC process.

A- Acknowledge that you are a sinner

B- Believe that Jesus Christ is the Son of God, and that Jesus died on the cross for your sin and arose from the dead on the third day, and

C- Confess this belief with your mouth.

"That if thou shalt confess with thy mouth the Lord Jesus, and shalt believe in thine heart that God hath raised him from the dead, thou shalt be saved. For with the heart man believeth unto righteousness: and with the mouth confession is made unto salvation…For whosoever shall call upon the name of the Lord shall be saved" (Romans 10:9-10, 13)

Prayer:

God, I come to you right now acknowledging that I am a sinner and have done wrong and horrible things in your sight. I know that I am not worthy to even come to you, but I believe that you sent your Son, Jesus Christ to die on the cross that my sins may be forgiven, and that Jesus arose from the dead on the third day. I ask you right now God, forgive me of my sins and come live in my heart so that I may not sin against you. Help me to desire to hunger and thirst after your Word, to learn more about who you are, and how I can live a life victorious in Jesus Christ. Thank you God for saving me. In the name of your Son, Jesus Christ. Amen.

Chapter 1

"MY STORY"

"Shit, shit, shit! I am mad as hell." As I sat on the sofa in the psychologist's office I was overwhelmed with anger. The very thought of the events of the morning and the past two weeks rushed back as a tape playing over and over in my mind. Here I sat, a distinguished Black woman with a Bachelor's degree in Psychology, an accomplished Howard University School of Divinity student, Master's graduate with a 3.8 GPA, and recipient of The W.O. Carrington Foundation Award, (an honor for the student who demonstrated a high degree of excellence in preparation and sermon delivery), characterized by exegetical and theological integrity; resorting to a four letter word to express her frustration and anger at the world for her current predicament.

Tears welled up in my eyes and I couldn't hold back nor hold it together any longer. I was mad at my daughter, I was mad at my other daughter, I was mad at my son, I was mad at my pastor, I was mad at my pastor's wife, I was mad at my family, I was mad at my church family, and I was mad at my ex-husband. I was mad at the people that seemed to have their lives altogether and were moving ahead with their God-given purpose. I was mad at the system of bureaucratic injustices. I was mad at the people that prey on the kindness and love of others. I was mad at people who victimize and abuse those that are less powerful, those that are oppressed, those that are hurting, those that are challenged, whether physically, mentally, or emotionally. I was mad at the world.

Why? Where do I begin? Most people often coin the phrase, "I'll begin at the beginning". Well, I am going to begin right where I am now, "*mad as hell*".

I whipped out my cell phone and called my therapist. "You've reached the voice mail...!" "She's not there either." All I could do was leave a message. "I need to see you NOW!" Ok, what do I do now? All of my theological training, all of my intellectual business training, all my psychological training, all my domestic violence training, everything I thought was supposed to get me from point A to point B was not working. My therapist was unavailable, and I was mad at everybody else, so who else could I call?

It's amazing how we often say in testimonies when people get in trouble and have problems; we walk our problems all over town. We call our girlfriends, we call our parents, our pastors, we call everybody but God. Well, don't you find it interesting that I was mad at everybody, but I never mentioned I was mad at God. I already had my bout with God about my predicament. It was only by the grace of God that I survived my abuse and the abuse of my children.

That was the beginning of it all. I am a conqueror of domestic violence and abuse. I was married for twenty-three years. Most of those years were plagued by domestic violence of some sort. You name it: verbal, emotional, marital rape, isolation, manipulation, economic, threats, and even the abuse of my children. It is only by God's mercy that I was not consumed. Only because God's compassion failed not, nor did God prove unfaithful to bring me out and bring me through. I have been walking in my deliverance for eight years. So, how did I end up here? Only God knew and I cried out to God.

Chapter 2

INTRODUCTION

Robert Walker in an opening sermon said, "In the sixty-eighth year of the first century there was an old man in a prison in Rome — a little circular cell about twenty feet in diameter — who was writing to a young man far across the Aegean and Adriatic Seas in Ephesus. The subject of his letter was how to keep strong in the midst of a collapsing civilization, and it seems an appropriate subject for us today. How can we stay strong in the midst of a collapsing civilization?" We are facing trouble on every hand and everywhere. The Christian believer is experiencing intense persecution and challenges far beyond his/her natural power to handle. *But understand this, that in the last days there will come times of stress. {2 Tim 3:1 RSV}*

I must note in passing, that the "last days" here is not referring to the final end time of the church on earth; but the last days include the whole period of time between the first and the second comings of Christ. From the very day that our Lord arose from the dead, these were the "last days." In these last days, Paul, an Apostle of Jesus Christ, said that there would come recurrent cycles of distress, some of which we are going through right now. Peace has forsaken the world and the world is in utter chaos; there are strange, demonic forces at work in society creating immense problems, and the family structure is declining.

We are in a syndrome of dangerous minds and dangerous times. Let us start by defining a syndrome? *A syndrome is a pattern of behavior that is chronic; recurring and usually unhealthy. It is defined as a group of signs and symptoms that occur together and characterize a particular abnormality.* The dangerous mind syndrome is not normal, it is not natural, and it is definitely not what God intends for God's children.

REALLY, dangerous minds are not something that scientists, psychologists, and psychiatrists have identified. Several newspaper articles, written by journalists in the Washington Post, were about the stories of 13 children that had been killed in May 2005. In the same newspaper, another article read: <u>*Murder in Mind; Psychologist Studies Brains of Serial Killers.*</u> For 30 years, Helen Morrison, a noted psychologist had been studying and probing the brains of serial killers. She interviewed them, visited them in prison, and even dissected their brains. At the conclusion of the article, she noted: "The question of why people do such terrible, inhuman things is still as intriguing to me as it was when I first started asking the question 30 years ago. Is there an answer? Not yet, there is no answer at all."

Through these times of distress in which we are living, we will see certain characteristics at play: *For men will be <u>lovers of self</u>, <u>lovers of</u> <u>money</u>, <u>proud</u>, <u>arrogant</u>, <u>abusive</u>, <u>disobedient to their parents</u>, <u>ungrateful</u>, <u>unholy</u>, <u>inhuman</u>, <u>not being able to be appeased or satisfied</u>, <u>slanderers</u>, <u>self-indulgent</u>, <u>fierce</u>, <u>haters of good</u>, <u>treacherous</u>, <u>reckless</u>, <u>swollen with</u> <u>conceit</u>, <u>lovers of pleasure rather than lovers</u> <u>of God</u>, <u>holding</u> <u>the form of</u> <u>religion but denying the power of it</u>. 2 Timothy 3:2-5a RSV*

We are living in perilous and dangerous times, so we have to recognize the dangerous mind syndrome. You may see it in someone you know, but you have to look beyond the behavior and see the malady itself. It becomes apparent that this syndrome does not impact only the young, and the elderly, but, it impacts men, women, and children of all ages, all races, all creeds, all sexual orientations, all classes, and all religions.

Dangerous minds are really about a state of mind, a view of life and a pattern of behavior that people hold on to that keeps them stuck and unable to progress. There are a lot of people, even in the body of Christ, who are stuck and unable to move forward. They are stuck in unhealthy relationships, unhealthy jobs, unhealthy eating habits, unhealthy living arrangements, unhealthy politics, unhealthy spending habits, unhealthy sexual appetites, and even unhealthy churches. Christian spiritual growth is dwarfed. Christians cannot become spiritually mature because they are stuck in the mentality that they can live their lives in a vacuum: separate, un-teachable, high minded, and apart from the body of Christ.

The failure to break the silence of unhealthy and unholy living practices are killing God's people daily. While the Holy Spirit will teach everything one needs to know, the bible says, *forsake not the assembling of yourselves (Hebrews 10:25).* Christianity is meant to be lived in fellowship and communion with one another. *For as we have many members in one body, and all members do not have the same office: so we, being many, are ONE BODY IN CHRIST and everyone members one of another (Romans 12:4-5).* There are no Lone Ranger Christians. The Lone Ranger had Tonto, Dorothy had Toto, Jack had Jill, Moses had Aaron, Naomi had Ruth, David had Jonathan, and Jesus had his twelve disciples.

Hosea 4:6, says, *My people are destroyed for lack of knowledge; because thou has rejected knowledge, I will also reject thee, that thou shalt be no priest to me: seeing thou hast forgotten the law of thy God, I will also forget thy children.*

Today there is a rapidly growing phenomenon that affects families across America and throughout the world. Each year, thousands of American children witness domestic violence within their families. Witnessing violence is a risk factor for long-term physical and mental health problems, including alcohol and substance abuse, being a victim of abuse, and becoming a perpetrator of domestic and intimate partner violence. Victims in many cases will go to their pastors, priests, or other lay leaders to disclose the abuse. Talking about the dynamics of domestic violence and abuse can help the faith community better understand the dynamics of violence and abuse, and give them the knowledge and resources to help facilitate the safety of victims of abuse.

Churches must recognize that all teaching is religious education that moves people towards their fullest potential and purpose of who God created them to be, and what God has called them to do. Religious education's purpose is to move one towards righteousness, justice, character, and knowledge. God created us all with the capacity to learn and be educated. Our lack of education will cause us to live undeveloped to the fullest potential and fullness of Jesus Christ, our head. The soul of the church has to be the liberation of all the people of God.

Defining Domestic Violence

Domestic violence is abusive behavior used by one person in an intimate relationship to maintain power and control over another. It is exerted through physical, psychological, and/ or economical means. As a consequence of severe intimate partner violence, female victims are more likely than male victims to need medical attention and take time from work; they also spend more days in bed and suffer more from stress and depression.[1]

The Maryland Network Against Domestic Violence report May 1999 statistics report:

1. The estimated yearly direct medical cost of caring for battered women is about $1.8 billion[2]
2. 75-85% of cases of abuse are women, with 15-25% being male victims
3. 1 out of every 4 American women (26%) report that they have been physically abused by husband or significant other
4. Every 15 seconds a woman is battered in the US, Between 50 – 70% of men who abuse their female partners abuse their children
5. At least 3.3 million children between the ages of 3 -19 are at risk of exposure to parental violence every year
6. About one-third of high school and college students experience violence in their intimate relationship during their dating years

The National Center For Victims of Crime report:

1. 1 violent crime is committed every 6 seconds
2. 1 rape/sexual assault every 2 minutes
3. 50 women are victimized by an intimate partner every hour
4. 1 teenager is victimized every 19 seconds
5. 3 people become victims of stalking every minute
6. 1 child is reported abused or neglected in America every 35 seconds

There are many myths about domestic violence and abuse which include the belief that physical battering is the only form of domestic violence, however, there are many forms of domestic violence.

Forms of domestic violence/intimate partner violence

Physical Abuse/Battering	Verbal Abuse	Sexual Abuse
Coercion	Isolation	Harassment
Threats	Economic Control	Marital Rape
Date Rape	Incest	Neglect or Withholding
Elder Abuse	Fratricide	Patricide
Homicide	Stalking	Sexual Assault

Paulo Freire speaks in his book, <u>Pedagogy of the Oppressed,</u> about violence and its effect of dehumanizing the victim. He says, *"dehumanization, which marks not only those whose humanity have been stolen, but also (though in a different way) those who have stolen it, as a distortion of the vocation of becoming more fully human."* Thus, people who are victims of domestic violence, struggle with trying to maintain humanity, recognizing that violence is an unjust order that is engendered in their oppressor (abuser). This leads the victims to struggle against their oppressors seeking to gain their own humanity and the humanity of their oppressor.

Domestic violence occurs in the home, school, work place, and church. It is a world-wide phenomenon that carries a stigma that forces many victims to live in silence and suffering.

Contributing Factors

The following is a list of contributing factors of domestic violence and abuse. While most experts believe they are not the root cause of violence and abuse, these issues can exert extraordinary influence over an abuser and can be a trigger that invokes the explosion phase in the cycle of abuse.

Financial Pressures (joblessness)	Power/Control	Anger
Victims Become Abusers	Mental Illness	Poor/Lack of Communication Skills
Culture	Misinterpretation of Scripture	Poor Parenting Skills
Dysfunctional/ deficient	Social System	Judicial System
Guilt/Shame	Desensitized Involvement	Drugs & Alcohol

Myths

People who do not understand nor have been educated about the dynamics of domestic violence and abuse have many misconceptions. You cannot believe everything you read and hear about domestic violence and abuse.

Common myths that are not true:

1. You can just leave
2. Only happens to the poor
3. Only happens in African-American population
4. To be kept a secret (family business)
5. She/he/I deserved it
6. Just pray about it
7. Christians should not seek professional counseling
8. It only happens to women and children
9. Physical battering is the only form of domestic violence

Ways (Remedies) to help and support victims and survivors of domestic violence:

Break the silence	Lobby for functioning legislative, judicial, & social governments
Dispel the myths	Parenting Classes
Promote Education	Become an Advocate
Professional Counseling	Financial Management Planning
Anger Management Counseling	Shelters/Safe Places

Safety Planning

It is extremely important for anyone suffering domestic violence and abuse to develop a safety plan. Statistics say it will take a victim to hear seven times they must leave an abusive relationship before they actually take steps to leave. Victims must also understand that the most crucial and unsafe time for them, is when they decide to leave their abuser. At the point of leaving, a victim is highly at risk of being killed.

Eventually, some victims do leave. The most important thing to let a victim know is that you want them to be safe, to have a safe place to go if they do decide to leave, and have a safety plan in place. *See Appendix A.*

1. Always call 911 at the onset of a violent and abusive episode
2. Let someone know outside immediate family
3. Develop safety signals with neighbors or friends
4. Copy all important papers, such as: car registration, birth certificates, social security cards, house deeds, school records, and health records
5. Clothes for 3-4 days
6. Cash put aside
7. Extra car and house keys
8. Always stay out of the kitchen and bathrooms

Cycle of Abuse

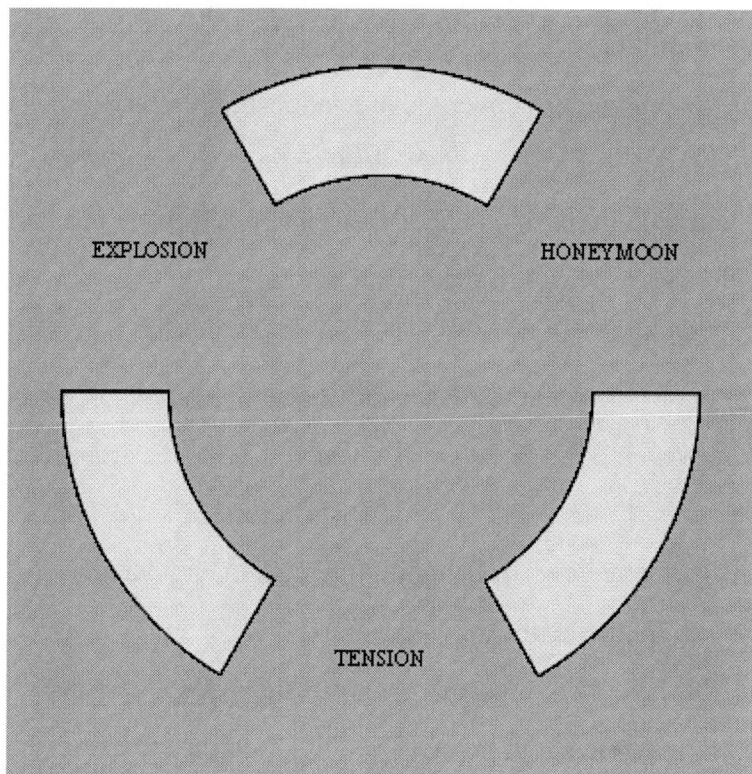

EXPLOSION   HONEYMOON

TENSION

Victims of domestic violence, especially those who are in physically abusive relationships, find themselves in a cycle of repeating actions.

There are three stages in this cycle of violence:

Honeymoon Stage

This is the beginning of every love relationship. Partners are very romantic, intense and seductive. Most victims remember these times and secretly wish and hope the relationship returns to the happier times as it was in the beginning.

Tension Stage

This phase of the cycle can last a day, a week, a month, or even years, however, once the cycle of violence begins it starts to occur more frequently. The tension building is described as feelings of unease, stress, feelings of being intimidated, manipulated, and threatened. In a relationship where abuse has been prevalent, a victim will come to know and recognize signs or triggers that cause an abuser to act violently. The victim will try to avoid any of these triggers. Sometimes, they will provoke the abuser in order to break the tension and get the abuse over with.

Explosion Stage

The violence or abuse occurs in this stage. It can be characterized by physical or sexual abuse, property destruction, heightened emotional abuse, abuse of animals, abuse of children, and even murder. The longer the abuse continues without intervention the more severe the abuse and violence becomes in order to maintain power and control.

(Taken from excerpts of "It Shouldn't Hurt to Go Home", Maryland Network Against Domestic Violence)

Once the explosion occurs, apologies, gifts, and promises that the abuse will never occur again are made by the abuser to change. Both the victim and abuser may minimize and rationalize the seriousness of the abuse and injuries. Self-condemnation or self -blame by the victim can occur by assuming the fault or cause of the abuse. The abuser will also place the blame of the abuse on the victim by alleging he/she provoked them to act violently. Once the reconciliation takes place, the victim feels this is a time of renewed courtship, romance, and sexual intimacy as it was in the beginning. However, if professional help has not been received, this is a false reconciliation and the abuse will continue. The cycle will begin again.

As mentioned earlier, there is nothing new under the sun. Many families in the Bible were as dysfunctional as families are today. Culture plays an important role in how family members are treated and how they act toward one another. There are patriarchal societies (father or male head of household), matriarchal societies (mother or female head of household), and societies where children are not very important- seen but not heard. Jesus broke through many of the boundaries that societies had set forth in the Old Testament and brought a New Testament of liberation to women, children, the hungry, the sick, the abused, and all that were oppressed. Paul, an Apostle of Jesus Christ, also broke through the ethnic, religious, and social boundaries of his day that separated the Jews from the Gentiles.

Fathers, mothers, and children were exposed to and experienced the hardships of living under tyrannical leadership and governments. Women and children, especially experienced the harsh realities of the power and control that were exerted over them. Not only do we find human to human abuse, but we also see how demonic forces caused turmoil and disruption in many homes (Matthew 15: 22- 28, Mark 5:1-16, Luke 9:38 – 42). Failure to believe and educate oneself about the evil and/or demonic forces that operate in the world through domestic violence and abuse leaves Christians exposed and vulnerable to the attacks of the enemy.

I pray that this book will help you to understand how the enemy, Satan, the devil , Lucifer, or whatever you choose to call the demonic forces operating in the world today, can and have attacked the children of God through domestic violence and abuse. Jesus, the master teacher, has left us instruction on how to impact and influence social change. One must be ready, willing, and able to suffer persecution, torture or even death, because they stand for righteousness, justice, and mercy——paralleling the suffering, persecution, and death of Christ. I pray that you realize that suffering and toil become meaningful because you have worked to improve the living conditions and lives of those who are oppressed and abused.

Notes

[1] National Research Council, 1996

[2] Wisner, et at. 1999

Chapter 3

"UNDER ATTACK"

We are in a spiritual war with the kingdom of darkness. We live behind enemy lines, and face the forces of Satan everyday.

2 Corinthians 10:3,4 ...for though we walk in the flesh, we do not war after the flesh: (For the weapons of our warfare are not carnal, but mighty through God to the pulling down of strong holds;)

A stronghold is an idea, a thought process, a habit, or an addiction through which Satan has set up occupancy in your life—- a place where he has the advantage.

What is spiritual warfare?

The enemy, a.k.a. the devil and Satan, uses strongholds to undermine the Christian believer to prevent them from living a victorious life in Jesus Christ, unless they are armed with the Word of God and prayer. The definition of spiritual warfare is, the conflict between the forces of God and the forces of Satan (demons), with the goal being the believer's victory in Christ. The bible reveals everything God wants you to know about spiritual warfare. Spiritual warfare is a threat to everyone, even the most fervent Christian. Satan will attack anyone—-especially those who believe that they are not vulnerable. If Satan can succeed in making the Christian feel a stigma attached to having demons, he may prevent that Christian from seeking deliverance.[1] These wicked spirits can invade and indwell a human body and/or inflict oppressive forces against the person to take control over their actions, behaviors, and thoughts.

Strongholds begin in your life when Satan gets a toe-hold in you, which is sometimes called, "open doors". The moment you start thinking that you are incapable of such behaviors as coveting, raging, entertaining lustful thoughts, jealousy, envying, and abuse, Satan will launch a surprise attack and try to trip you in the area you feel most impenetrable.[2] There are many names for Satan as found in the Scriptures: the wicked one, the deceiver, the destroyer, the adversary, the enemy of our souls, the prince of the power of the air. All of the previous descriptions of Satan are from Scriptures. Satan appears as a proper name in the Old Testament, referring to the super-human enemy of God, humanity, and good. (1 Chronicles 21:1)

In the New Testament, the enemy is referred to as the tempter, the evil one, the prince of this world, the god of this age, the strong man, the accuser of our brothers. The following scriptures can help you in your studies: (John 12:31, 2 Corinthians 4:4, 1 Thessalonians 3:5, Matthew 12: 29, Matthew 13:19, 38, and Revelation 12:10.) Satan's power is so great that Michael the archangel viewed him as a foe too powerful to oppose (Jude 9). Satan is a highly intelligent being, and I John 5:19 declares, *"The whole world is under the control of the evil one."*[3] Nevertheless, God is stronger than the enemy and has given us characteristics to help identify the enemy for who and what he is*: a liar, a murderer, a sower of discord, an adversary, cunning, wicked, malignant – totally evil, cowardly, a tempter, a thief, without principles, proud, deceitful, fierce and cruel, aggressive, and a destroyer.*[4]

There are times when become so overwhelmed by the tactics of the enemy that we feel powerless. In domestic abuse, victims often feel powerless over their lives and the lives of their families. We will look at the manifestations of demonic forces in comparisons to the types/forms of domestic violence and abuse, and the symptoms and signs in children who have been abused. We shall explore how Satan uses means to lead people to sin and how these actions and behaviors lead to open doors for Satan and his demonic forces to enter into the lives of victims.

Some people do not believe that Satan and demons exist, but through my own experiences, and mainly through the written Word of God, it is made plain that Satan does exist and that his main work is to oppose God's rule in the events and the lives of God's people. This war began in the Garden of Eden when Satan's cunning lies tricked Adam and Eve and took over their rule of the world (**Genesis 3:1-5**).

All of the Gospels in the New Testament record Jesus cleansing the temple. Jesus was filled with righteous indignation at what He found in the temple. At once, Jesus began to take action and clean out everything that was defiling the temple of God. Clearly, in my understanding, Jesus was mad ~~as~~ at hell. With the same righteous indignation and fervor that Jesus cleansed the temple of God, we must counter attack anything that would defile our temples (our bodies).

*What? know ye not that your body is the temple of the Holy Ghost which is in you, which ye have of God, and ye are not your own? For ye are bought with a price: therefore glorify God in your body, and in your spirit, which are God's. **1 Corinthians 6:19-20***

This book is intended to educate, equip, and empower you towards seeking deliverance. It is strongly recommended for you to do further study and to seek out help from those in ministry that have the Gifts of the Spirit that work in deliverance ministries. The bible says in 2 Timothy 2:15, "*Study to shew thyself approved unto God, a workman that needeth not to be ashamed, rightly dividing the word of truth.*" (See Appendix B for a list of books recommended for reading on further study of Spiritual Warfare).

Satan is an unwanted trespasser and thief. As the head of your family or spiritual leader of your family, you are responsible for attending to the affairs of your family. You are responsible for addressing the issues or problems that may occur as a result of things that may have happened within your family. You have the ability to exert power, authority, influence, intellect, and intelligence over Satan and his demons to evict them.

The evil one has your name, address, phone numbers (home, work, cell, fax) email address, social security number, rank, status, and class. He will call you up at the most inopportune times. He, along with other demonic forces, arrive unannounced at your front door, demand to come in and sit down, expect you to feed them, and will never go home. You may evict them one day, but be assured they will come back the next day, the next month, the next year, demand your undivided attention, sit on your sofa with you, eat your popcorn, watch your television, and bring other unwanted guests with them (more demons).

When the unclean spirit is gone out of a man, he walketh through dry places, seeking rest; and finding none, he saith, I will return unto my house whence I came out. And when he cometh, he findeth it swept and garnished. Then goeth he, and taketh to him seven other spirits more wicked than himself; and they enter in, and dwell there: and the last state of that man is worse than the first. **Luke 11:24-26**

Notes

1 Pigs in the Parlor, pp. 22
2 The Disciple's Victory, pp. 10
3 The Disciple's Victory, p. 11
4 The Strongman's His Name, p. 2

Chapter 4

"HER STORY"

"And, behold, a woman of Canaan came out of the same coasts, and cried unto him, saying, Have mercy on me, O Lord, thou Son of David; my daughter is grievously vexed with a devil" . **Matthew 15:22**

"For a certain woman, whose young daughter had an unclean spirit, heard of him, and came and fell at his feet: The woman was a Greek, a Syrophenician by nation; and she besought him that he would cast forth the devil out of her daughter." **Mark 7:25-26**

We find in these texts a story of a woman who has a daughter being grievously vexed by a devil. If we look inside her home and take a closer look at what goes on in her household, we will discover what happens when a child is troubled with a devil or has an unclean spirit. The book of Mark differs in his telling of the story in that he says the daughter was possessed by a devil and it needed to be cast forth out of her.

Note: Whether one is possessed or oppressed by a devil, you are going to get the same results. The same characteristics will manifest themselves because a devil is a devil, is a devil.

Manifested Characteristics

Demons are permitted to afflict a person with bodily diseases, tempt humans with unclean thoughts and vary in degrees of wickedness. They instigate rulers and authorities (i.e., fathers, mothers and other authority figures) to wage war against others, and those who are afflicted with a demon. The devil or unclean spirit, expresses the mind and consciousness of the demon/devil/unclean spirit that is dwelling in them or oppressing them.

We cannot be led astray or be caught up with the semantics of whether one is possessed or oppressed by a devil, but realize and acknowledge that demon activity is going on in our homes. The books (Luke 8 and Mark 5) give us characteristics of the demoniac who was possessed with a legion of demons. Please read and study these scriptures thoroughly to get a complete understanding of behaviors. Perhaps you recognize some of these behaviors in your own home.

Act	Associated Behaviors
confusion	unable to make decisions, second guessing self
disruption	not able to meet goals, procrastination
chaos	disoriented, inability to focus
cursing & swearing	arguments, innapropriate language, verbal abuse
manipulation	blaming, invoking guilt
violence & fighting	physical abuse
lying, killing, stealing	destroying property, stealing cars, goods
tears & throws in the fire	self mutilation, cutting oneself
dwells in tombs	dark places, wears black colors
cannot be contained, wild	disobedient, no respect for adults, authority
abusing themselves	body piercing, tattoos, drinking, drugs, unsafe sex
wears no clothes	skimpy outfits, no covering of one's body
driven into the wilderness	running away from home, home is not a safe place
suicide	depression, no hope, powerless, life unbearable to live

Chapter 5

"THE NOW MOMENT"

God reminded me of his promises and His Word. I began to pray every passage of scripture I knew about God's promises, God's faithfulness, God's peace, and God's deliverance in times of trouble. What I received was God's strength to help me make it through another day. The anger, the hurt, and the resentments were not removed from me, but God gave me the strength to move into the "now moment" the kairos, the appointed time. This is the time when God knows it is the right time. This is the time of opportunities, moments that are God ordained, and appointments with God. It is knowing that everything I have been through was for an appointed time. It is a time when we must humble ourselves and our ideas to the wisdom and power of God and trust Him when He says He will not be late. (Appointed time also means a time already established and decided for certain reasons) It is like having an appointment. You can't get in until the appointment time, and that is just the way it is. God has set appointments for us concerning certain issues in our lives, so we might as well settle down, be patient and wait for the appointed time to come. It will not happen until then. Your purpose has an appointed time. There are things that God has ordained to happen before your purpose can be fulfilled.

It is a time that discernment must kick in and you must seek to see what is not apparent to the natural eye. It is the time that you have to demonstrate that you are awake and know it is your time to move. No more complacency, no more procrastination, no more running in vicious cycles. It is now time to take action.

> *I said in mine heart, God shall judge the righteous and the wicked: for there is a time for every purpose and for every work* ***Ecclesiastes 3:17***.

I had arrived at my final breaking point. I had been ministering to and struggling with my children for the past ten years surrounding their abuse. Recently, my daughter had a breakthrough and broke her silence publicly about her abuse. So, why was I at this point? I felt like Elijah after his victory at Mt. Carmel against the four hundred fifty prophets of Baal. Elijah was victorious, God had shown Himself strong over the false prophets, the evil forces of the enemy, and Elijah ran off and hid in a cave (I Kings 18-19).

How can God give you such victory one moment and the next moment you feel like the rug has been snatched from underneath you? I believe that it's because God is moving you into higher heights and deeper depths in the things of God. God has a desire for you to continue in your growth to spiritual maturity and understand the whole truth of your existence. Elijah's work was not done. My daughter's testimony was not the end of my journey with abuse. God had another assignment for me, another appointment to meet. But, what now God? What more can I do? I can imagine God saying, "Glad you asked!"

Chapter 6

"THE JOURNEY CONTINUES"

Due time had arrived. Due time is when God knows you are ready, when everyone else involved is ready, and when it fits into God's corporate plan. God has individual plans for your life, but He also has a corporate plan for the entire world. It is up to you to give your will over to God for His purposes.

> *The Lord is not slack concerning His promise, as some men count slackness; but is longsuffering to usward, not wiling that any should perish, but that all should come to repentance.* **2 Peter 3:9**

God's due time is here. I had to recognize that God was not finished with me yet. I was reminded that everything has an end, including each one of our lives. If we look at the effects of domestic violence in the lives of a family, we will see the dynamics and interactions within that family is like experiencing death. Grief, anxiety, separation, and loss are prevailing feelings. Psychiatrist Elisabeth Kubler-Ross has provided us with a theory that people who learn of their impending death or death of loved ones tend to pass through five distinct stages: denial, anger, bargaining, depression, and acceptance.[1] Velma Stevens, an author who has been twice widowed, in her book, *Grief Work,* lists the following emotions:

shock, disbelief, numbness, sorrow, loss of meaning, anger, hostility guilt, fear, loneliness, depression, acceptance, resignation, and peace. She does not suggest a time sequence of stages for these emotions, although a process of working through them is evident.[2]

Experiencing the grief, transition, and loss of my own marriage and the destruction of my family in the after-effects of the domestic abuse, I can attest to these feelings. As Velma Stevens suggests, there is no time sequence of the stages. I have experienced the shock, disbelief, numbness, sorrow, loss of meaning, guilt, fear, loneliness, and depression. "Bam!" The anger and hostility had set in. My appointed time of anger had arrived. God knew that I had more work to do. You have heard the phrase, "sick and tired of being sick and tired". Well, it is not until we reach that point, have we had enough. Enough of the hurt, enough of the pain, enough of the enough. There is a popular movie with Jennifer Lopez called, "Enough." Like Jennifer, she had had enough of an abusive husband and she was moved to action. She was called to handle her predicament in the way she thought was best.

God's due time is the time for Christian believers to understand the spiritual implications of domestic violence and abuse. I had to reach my appointed time to take action and start the healing process for women, men, and children who have experienced the traumatic events of domestic violence and abuse. Breaking the silence of the spiritual forces, the demonic activity that is taking place in our lives, and coming to terms that Satan and demons do exist is long overdue. Silence and reluctance to talk about such matters, I realized, was a great risk to my self-disclosure for some and my reputation to others, but I had to obey God rather than man.

Notes

[1] Psychology an Introduction, pp. 317-318
[2] Grief, Transition, and Loss, pp. 40

Chapter 7

"THE STRONGMAN HAD SET UP HIS FORTRESS"

Understanding the developmental vulnerabilities of children from infancy to old age is important to understanding the responses we give to the experiences we face in life. Children love imitating their parents. Many of us have played house during our childhood. We pretended that we were a husband or wife and children living as a make believe family. Playing house can be healthy, but I have come to understand that playing house can be unhealthy. The degree to which children imitate their parents can lead to domestic violence and abuse. For me, at a very early age, around seven or eight I was introduced to sex by playing house.

At the age of eighteen, I was date raped, became pregnant, and had an abortion. I did not consider my experience at the age of eighteen rape, because it was my boyfriend, and the truth be told, I was somewhere I should not have been, so I suffered in silence.

Now, I was forty years old, had been married for twenty years, and I was mother of three children, two daughters (ages eighteen and fourteen), and a son (seven years old). I was a successful business woman, a manager at Bell Atlantic (now Verizon) and was required to travel several days out of the month. I was making a good salary that was enough to support my entire household. I was the major breadwinner in the family, a Christian and very active in my church. At that time, I had a call on my life to be a preacher of the gospel. My husband, who was also my abuser, (at that time) was unemployed and would occasionally find jobs here and there. Most of his money was being made by selling drugs. He was a habitual user of marijuana as well. My life was a living hell with verbal, emotional, and sexual abuse. The travel that was required by my job was a welcome escape from the abuse, but it was to the detriment of my children. When I was traveling, he would abuse them. Unfortunately, I was ignorant of the fact that there was something called domestic violence going on in my life. Because my abuser was my husband, I did not consider the sexual abuse as marital rape.

My people are destroyed for lack of knowledge: because thou has rejected knowledge, I will also reject thee, that thou shalt be no priest to me: seeing thou hast forgotten the law of thy God, I will also forget thy children. **Hosea 4:6**

My upbringing in a Christian home and the misinterpretation of scripture kept me in an abusive relationship. I was taught that the husband is the head of the household and had conjugal rights (marital privileges) over his wife. This is what a wife is "supposed" to do. There were many times he would come in from wherever he was coming from and would want to have sex. I wouldn't want to, so he'd force it. I can recall times after the sex, I would get in the shower and literally try to scrub my skin off, trying to remove his touch and his smell. He would also play the mind games on me by heating up irons during arguments. I would immediately give in. I suffered under the hands of my abusive husband for many years. I did this to try and keep my family together.

My youngest daughter had become unmanageable: running away from home, cutting school, being disrespectful at home to both me and her father. While away on one of my trips, my youngest daughter was raped. She was taken to counseling and during one of her sessions she disclosed that her father had been sexually abusing her. It was determined that my older daughter had also experienced the abuse before she went off to college. October, 1993 I was called into the ministry. February, 1994 I preached my initial sermon. September, 1995 I felt like I had hit rock bottom.

The bottom had fallen out of my life. Our abuser was removed from our home and was prohibited to have any contact with his daughters. Their father refused to provide any support to the family. I was left alone raising three children, in school, one daughter in college, one in and out of treatment facilities and hospitals, and a son who was too young to really understand what was going on. My oldest daughter dropped out of college and became pregnant. Our entire family was in counseling, trying to piece our lives back together.

My daughters have suffered a great deal of emotional distress. I later found out that my youngest daughter had experienced the severest of the abuse and for a longer period of time. On several occasions she tried to commit suicide. She became sexually promiscuous, drank, and smoked, and was constantly running away from home. The only thing I could do was consistently call in a missing child report. She dropped out of school because she could not handle school. She also experienced black-outs and could not focus nor concentrate. I was in and out of courts and hospitals, while trying to work to support my family, maintain my job, go to school, and work in the ministry.

I was devastated. I watched my entire world fall apart. Where was I to turn? How could I make it? All I wanted, I thought; was the American dream: a family with children, a house, and a job that would give us the financial freedom to live better than how I had grown up. I wanted to bring glory and honor to God in everything I did, knowing that God would bless my efforts and good intentions. I wanted my children to be successful, married, and to live their lives to the fullest potential and purpose that God had created them for.

As I sat in that chair at the doctor's office, I realized that I wasn't mad at the people in my life. I wasn't mad at the circumstances nor the actual events and trials I had faced in my life time. I wasn't even mad **as** hell, but I was mad **at** hell. In other words, I had finally come to understand the evil events, life circumstances, and even the choices we make are sometimes influenced by satanic and demonic forces that exist in our world today. I realized the devil is strong (strongman) and relentless. Satan has no respect of person and will use anyone and anything to thwart the work of God and render God's people ineffective, upset, and confused.

As a believer in Christ, you must understand that you struggle against the world, the flesh, and the devil. Any attitude or action done without total dependence on God will render the believer helpless and powerless over these demonic influences. Conversely, we have victory over the enemy because Jesus triumphed over Satan and his demonic forces in Jesus' death and resurrection (Colossians 2:15). I recognized my battle was not a physical battle, but my battle was spiritual in nature, and the weapons that I was going to have to use were not weapons of the world.

For though we walk in the flesh, we do not war after the flesh: (For the weapons of our warfare are not carnal, but mighty through God to the pulling down of strong holds;) Casting down imaginations, and every high thing that exalteth itself against the knowledge of God, and bring-

ing into captivity every thought to the obedience of Christ; And having in a readiness to revenge all disobedience, when your obedience is fulfilled. **2 Corinthians 10:3-6**

You must believe that the spiritual battle you face in domestic violence and the way it manifests itself in your life can be overcome. You must understand and believe that the weapons that God has provided you to use in this spiritual battle have the divine power to demolish the strongholds the strongman has set up in your life. In the scripture above, the promise in the verse is that you have the power to take all thoughts captive and to make them obedient to Christ.

The strongholds that can manifest in your life can be classified under three categories: (Excerpt definitions taken from Avery Willis, MasterLife - The Disciple's Victory)

Personal Strongholds – areas of our lives in which we are most vulnerable to Satan's or the strongman's attacks. These areas are where Satan always "seems" to get an advantage over you. These attacks are through the <u>flesh</u>, your inner tendency and capacity to sin. Through the flesh you can be influenced in your mind, your will, and your emotions. Your pride can sometimes keep you in bondage. Satan wants you to depend on yourself and your own strength. We can do it ourselves, we don't need help from anybody. We can just pray it away. I am a strong believer in prayer, but God has given us other tools and Spiritual Gifts in the body of Christ to work in conjunction with prayer. Ephesians 4:27 says, *"Neither give place to the devil."* Don't let Satan have an inch, a toehold, or the slightest chance of influencing you. The slightest inch, or toehold will become a stronghold in your life before you know it.

Ideological Strongholds- are built around systems of thought and ideas that are embodied in cultures and that exert pressure on members of that culture. Through this influence, which the bible calls the <u>world,</u> a whole society begins to hold certain values. What Satan does to individuals through the flesh, he does in society through the world. In time, personal strongholds become embodied in cultures as strongholds.

Tolerance of domestic abuse has become a stronghold in the lives of victims as well as in our societies. Domestic violence and abuse is a worldwide phenomenon. Many Christians encounter claims of intolerance when they take a stand against such issues as: pornography, homosexuality, abortion, gambling, the religious revolution which has embraced other world religions, separation/divorce, and other marital and relational issues of abuse. Paul warns us in Colossians 2:8, not to be deceived by deceptive philosophies that were born out of human traditions and principles of world systems rather than on Christ. Our religious, philosophical, value, economic, educational, and political systems have clouded our society's sense of right and wrong.

Cosmic Strongholds – the actual attack of Satan and a group of evil spirits that, with the aid of humanity, establishes a counter-culture of sin defying God's righteous order. Its goal is to oppose God's work and to steal, kill, and destroy. In the world around us- in the atmosphere- are evil beings under Satan's leadership. During our seminary class, we held discussions that claimed evil spirits were psychological states of mind. The devil was dismissed as a general force or thought that represented evil natural forces in humanity. Well, you can believe that if you like, but just like I believe that God's presence was with me in the midst of my suffering, failure, and disappointment and delivered me from my abuse; I believe and have seen demonic forces and influences manifest themselves. It is through my own moral integrity and notions that I attribute divine meaning and character to God and God's dispensation of mercy, justice, kindness, goodness, holiness, righteousness, blessedness, truth, and love during the presence of my domestic violence experiences. During the latter years of the 20th century, Satan's forces have gained so many strong-holds in the United States that Americans are acknowledging and have begun to be aware of evil spirits, the occult, mediums, chan-neling, demon possession, and satanic worship[1]. I also witnessed a well known talk show host, Oprah Winfrey, interviewing witch-es as they openly talked about their work.

For we wrestle not against flesh and blood, but against principalities, against powers, against the rulers of the darkness of this world, against spiritual wickedness in high places **Ephesians 6:12**

The atmosphere seems to be the abode of various kinds of spiritual beings that fight against the cause of God and of Christ. You must begin to define your battleground and what is happening in your life. Many of you have experienced unexplainable behavior, actions, and circumstances in your life that you cannot comprehend. But a word of caution, upon examining your experiences, bring your experiences in line with the Word of God and avoid interpreting the Bible to fit your experiences. Also, remember that Christ has already won the victory over the flesh, the world, and the devil. You need to claim your victory and exalt Christ, because it is only through Christ that you can win the victory.

Notes

[1] The Disciple's Victory, p. 20

Chapter 8

"DEFINING YOUR BATTLEGROUND"

I received Christ at an early age, but like many of us who profess the name of Christ, I strayed away from all that my parents, pastors, and teachers had taught me about living the Christian life. I was a teenager that wanted to live my life the way I wanted to and as a result, I opened many doors to Satan that gave him authority to operate in my life. I was what my mother called, "smelling myself" and doing my own thing. I lost my virginity at the age of sixteen. My rebellion to my parents' teaching and God's commandments not only put me in harms way, but it also started a chain of events that perpetuated in the lives of my daughters. Because of shame and guilt, I kept silent about my abuse and it allowed the demonic forces to continue their activity in my life for over twenty years.

I returned to being actively involved in my church and trying to grow spiritually after the first year of my marriage. Even before I was married, during the dating stages of my relationship with my husband, the signs of abuse were there. I was ignorant of what the signs meant. Oh, if only I had known then what I know now, I could have avoided the hurt, pain was embarking on a marvelous practical application of God's total divine plan for my deliverance, and only God was going to be able to free me from the bondage and slavery that my life had become.

As I continued my search, below the meaning of the number thirteen was the definition for the Thirteenth Amendment of the U.S. Constitution. It reads:

> *An amendment to the U.S. Constitution providing that "neither slavery nor involuntary servitude will exist in the United States and giving Congress the power to enforce this article of legislation.*

Hallelujah!!! I was shouting in my spirit. That's it. Domestic violence and abuse enslaves one to the power and control of another. But, we have the power and authority to enforce God's commandments of freedom and liberty in our lives. Through my deliverance, I am mandated to educate, equip, and empower (E^3) the believers to know and understand that they too have the authority and power to kick Satan out of their lives. How could I find consolation, justice, and hope in living out my life now, realizing the trauma, degradation, and humiliation I experienced at the hands of my abusers? How could I go on living under the choices I had willingly made in my life?

> *This I recall to mind, therefore I have hope. It is of the Lord's mercies that we are not consumed, because his compassions fail not. They are new every morning; great is thy faithfulness.* **Lamentations 3:21-23**

and devastation I experienced. Nevertheless, in my quest for knowledge, I was drawn to books about spiritual warfare. Once I had rededicated my life to Christ, and truly knew and understood what living a life victorious in Christ meant, I started having dreams. I awakened with visions of shadows and evil presences all about me. I awakened one night with the appearance of a giraffe head hanging over my bed. My son was plagued by terrible nightmares at the age of two. Every night I would have to go to his room and read bible stories or one book in particular called, "By Jesus' Thirty-nine Stripes You Were Healed". This book consisted of thirty-nine scripture verses from the bible that promised healing to the believer. I would faithfully read this book to my son. I can't remember when the nightmares stopped, but they stopped.

I became interested in understanding spiritual warfare and demonic forces, so I started reading some very popular books by Frank Perriti entitled, *This Present Darkness, and Piercing the Darkness*. These books dealt with the personal, ideological, and cosmic strongholds that were perceived in a town. It was amazing to read how the evil spiritual forces were controlling many of the events that were happening in this town. I thirsted for more and more knowledge about spiritual warfare and demonic forces. I would align the Bible next to me as I read various books about spiritual warfare. I would compare what was in the Bible to the events and circumstances surrounding various activities portrayed in the books. Years passed and I was always cognizant of things that appeared as strange happenings around me. What I failed to realize was that many of the things I was experiencing in my own life were stepping stones to Satan setting up his fortress in my life.

Personal Strongholds (that had been established in my life included):

Bitterness	Speech	Anxiety	Rejection
Un-Forgiveness	Date Rape	Loneliness	Pride
Fornication	Guilt	Sexual Abuse	Marital Rape
Teenage Pregnancy	Shame	Poor Parenting Skills	Fear

Ideological Strongholds:

Domestic Violence	Political Systems	Abortion	Incest
Child Abuse	Idolatry	Economic/ Financial Systems	Judicial System
Marriage	False Religious Teachers	Divorce	Social Systems

Cosmic Strongholds:

Confusion	Manipulation	Depression	Oppression	Isolation
Grief	Verbal Abuse	Threats	Emotional Abuse	Coercion

As you can see, those who wrestle with personal strongholds also need to fight the ideological systems of the world so that they can live holy lives and fulfill God's mission for the believer in the world. Fists, guns, knives, and other weapons can cause physical harm, but rape, abuse, manipulation, threats, and isolation can cause emotional harm. Logic, physical efforts, positive thinking, and psychological tactics will not win the battle over Satan. Only the spiritual weapons that God gives can help you win spiritual victories.

Tearing down strongholds is not easy and you will encounter claims that threaten to undermine your faith, and you will experience thoughts that do not honor Christ. But, you must persevere. Your knowledge and understanding fueled by the Holy Spirit will give you wisdom to combat the forces working against God's plan and purpose for your life (Proverbs 4:7, 16:16, Colossians 1:9, 4:5, James 1:5). Learn to listen and invoke the ministry of presence with God. Do not let what I called E^3 (experience, education, and ego) get in the way of your humility. God is the example of unconditional love and how to share His love with others. When all the words, experiences, and knowledge of what you have tried, (worldly wisdom), have failed you and you don't know what to do; listening for God instructions may be your answer.

Always, always seek God first. Sometimes I think I am not to seek God because God has given me the Word, experiences, and learning to deal with life. I must seek God to know how to apply it to every situation. As I began defining the battleground and territory that Satan had conquered in my life, either through doors I opened or doors that were thrust open by others, I was amazed and in awe. There were a total of thirteen (13) demonic forces that were identified. Now the number thirteen by our culture is not a good number. I hesitate to say unlucky number, because my Christian belief is that nothing is by luck nor chance. Nevertheless, I had to understand this for myself.

Webster's Ninth Collegiate Dictionary did not have a definition for the number thirteen, other than a reference to the number table. The internet encyclopedia defines thirteen as:

> Thirteen is regarded as an unlucky number in many cultures. One (probably unverifiable) theory holds that 13 is a reflection of the human fear of the unknown, since it is the first number that cannot be enumerated by using our 10 fingers and 2 feet. Unreasoned fear of the number 13 is termed triskaidekaphobia. Due to this fear, some tall buildings have resorted to skipping the "thirteenth floor", simply by numbering it "14" (though it's really still the

thirteenth floor) or by designating the floor "12a" or similar instead. The thirteenth of a month is likewise ominous, particularly when it falls on a Friday (see Friday the 13th). The 13th falls on a Friday more often than any other day. In fact it occurs more often than any other day/number combination except those that coincide with it (Thursday the 12th, Saturday the 14th, etc).[1]

We have also heard 'the thirteenth hour', signifying that a solution or help has occurred too late. I could not accept these meanings as God's answer for me. Many Christians know that numbers have significant meaning in the bible. Thus, I searched the ABC's of the bible and much to my chagrin the number explanation stopped at twelve; signifying twelve being the perfect number. So I went to the New Lexicon Webster's Dictionary of the English Language seeking some hope that my suffering of thirteen demonic spirits was not in vain. Lexicon says: 'being one more than twelve; ten plus three'.

The significance of ten in the bible is the number with a marvelous practical application, such as counting with the ten fingers which led to the decimal system, it also represents the sum of the sacred numbers 3 and 7, and the complete perfection as in the Ten Commandments. The number three represents totality. The universe consists of heaven, earth, and under the earth. Noah had three sons, who are the ancestors of all people. Three also is the Sacred Trinity of The Father, The Son, and The Holy Ghost. Now, I was getting somewhere. My revelation was that I was embarking on a marvelous practical application of God's total divine plan for my deliverance, and only God was going to be able to free me from the bondage and slavery that my life had become.

As I continued my search, below the meaning of the number thirteen was the definition for the Thirteenth Amendment of the U.S. Constitution. It reads:

An amendment to the U.S. Constitution providing that "neither slavery nor involuntary servitude will exist in the United States and giving Congress the power to enforce this article of legislation.

Hallelujah!!! I was shouting in my spirit. That's it. Domestic violence and abuse enslaves one to the power and control of another. But, we have the power and authority to enforce God's commandments of freedom and liberty in our lives. Through my deliverance, I am mandated to educate, equip, and empower (E^3) the believers to know and understand that they too have the authority and power to kick Satan out of their lives. How could I find consolation, justice, and hope in living out my life now, realizing the trauma, degradation, and humiliation I experienced at the hands of my abusers? How could I go on living under the choices I had willingly made in my life?

This I recall to mind, therefore I have hope. It is of the Lord's mercies that we are not consumed, because his compassions fail not. They are new every morning; great is thy faithfulness. **Lamentations 3:21-23**

God's unmerited favor was with me. I cried unto the Lord, and He heard me and delivered me out of a horrible pit, and set my feet upon a rock (Jesus); and established me going and coming. I encourage you to read the entire chapter 3 of Lamentations, "A Prophet's Anguish" and "A Prophet's Hope".

Let's look at my life and the personal, ideological, and cosmic strongholds the demonic forces had set up.

1. Spirit of Divination (Rebellion, magic, horoscopes, souvenirs, hypnosis)

*For rebellion is as the sin of witchcraft, and stubbornness is as iniquity and idolatry. Because thou hast rejected the word of the Lord, he hath also rejected thee from being king. **1 Samuel 15:23***

One of the most profound issues that we all deal with is rebellion and stubbornness. In the very beginning in the Garden of Eden, sin was conceived in the world through an act of disobedience and rebellion against God's commandment. Adam was told not to eat of the fruit of the tree of knowledge of good and evil.

*And the Lord God commanded the man, saying, Of every tree of the garden thou mayest freely eat: But of the tree of the knowledge of good and evil, thou shalt not eat of it: for in the day that thou eatest thereof thou shalt surely die. **Genesis 2:16-17***

When we define sin, it is defined as rebellion against God's commandments. Instead of us choosing to live our lives God's way, we choose to live our lives by our own standards, beliefs and values. Often those standards do not match up with God's will for our lives. Think about it. Did you seek God for your spouse? Did you seek God for your career path or education path? How many of you go to God with your problems first, before walking them all over town to your friends, family, and therapists? Many of us have stubbornly refused to give God His rightful place in our lives. Even resisting submission to the authority and rule of those who God have set in place to have the rule over you is rebelling against God. Too bad I had to learn this the hard way as well. I didn't seek God for my spouse and look what I ended up with.

God desires for us to seek Him in every area of our lives. Instead, we march our problems around the world seeking answers through prophets, fortunetellers, do it yourself helps, spiritualists, friends, and family members. Examination of literature suggests by and large that therapy or counseling have not been adequately utilized by African American people to deal with their problems. In fact, African-descent people are more likely to rely on traditional support networks (relatives, grandmothers, ministers) during times of stress, anxiety, and tension.[2] Only when the problems reach a certain level of severity will Black Americans seek help outside of their traditional support networks. In a 1991 National Survey of

Black Americans, it was reported that there was a greater likelihood of Black Americans to seek help for a physical ailment outside of their traditional support network. It was also reported that less than half of over 1300 respondents sought help outside their traditional support network when it was related to a personal problem.

Recognizing that many people look to their faith leaders and include them as a part of their support system, it is important that faith leaders are educated to the dynamics of domestic violence and abuse. It was only under the guidance of my pastor that I was able to walk away free from my abuser. So we must be able to integrate our faith and the professional guidance of those who God has called to such a task of counseling those in abusive relationships. It is imperative to select a professional counselor that is able to integrate your faith beliefs into your counseling.

Nevertheless, we stubbornly refuse to give God the authority and Jesus Lordship of our lives. I rebelled against my parents as I grew older, refusing to obey their authority. I wanted to do my own thing and get married, thinking I was going to live happily ever after. I really didn't understand the commandment, "children obey your parents". Our parents' wisdom, no matter how old we get or how old they get, is to be treasured and respected. "If only I had listened!"

The wisdom of the world is not the best place to seek God's answers for your life. The Book of Jeremiah says it like this:

> *For thus saith the Lord of hosts, the God of Israel; Let not your*
> *prophets and your diviners, that be in the midst of you, deceive you, nei-*
> *ther hearken to your dreams which ye cause to be dreamed. For they*
> *prophesy falsely unto you in my name: I have not sent them, saith the*
> *Lord. For thus saith the Lord, That after seventy years be accomplished*
> *at Babylon I will visit you, and perform my good word toward you, in*
> *causing you to return to this place. For I know the thoughts that I think*
> *toward you, saith the Lord, thoughts of peace, and not of evil, to give*
> *you an expected end.* **Jeremiah 29:8-11**

The doors to the spirit of divination were opened when I was a child
and continued into my adulthood. Who would have thought the innocent
act of a parent taking their children to magic shows was harmful?
Another door was opened through horoscopes. Now, I never allowed the
horoscopes to control my life; but you can read in the daily newspapers,
magazines and other literature what the stars say about your personality,
and character. Mostly women and some men believe in astrology and let
it run their lives. If you ask anyone today, nearly eight in ten Americans
will be able to tell you what sign they were born under.[3]

Many of you have traveled to foreign countries and love to bring
back relics and souvenirs from those countries. To my horror I learned
that some of the items can carry evil spirits in them. Anything you purchase you want to be sure you know what you are buying, such as: paint-

ings, artifacts, statues, and graven images. These things may be idols representing various gods and have spirits attached to them. Well, when I read about these things, I immediately went through my house and started denouncing, throwing away and purging everything that I thought might remotely resemble an idol or item that could have spirits attached to them. Even some very sentimental pieces that I received from my mother -who is now deceased - had to go. It was tough parting with some of the pieces, but I had to pray and ask God for guidance. My conclusion was: sometimes parents just don't know any better and have lived their lives to the best of their knowledge. Well, I threw everything away, anointed my house, asked God's forgiveness and I asked for God's guidance for any future purchases.

> *The graven images of their gods shall ye burn with fire: thou shalt not desire the silver or gold that is on them, nor take it unto thee, lest thou be snared therein: for it is an abomination to the Lord thy God. Neither shalt thou bring an abomination into thine house, lest thou be a cursed thing like it: but thou shalt utterly detest it, and thou shalt utterly abhor it; for it is a cursed thing. Deuteronomy 7:25-26*

Hypnosis is another area where you need to proceed with caution. Hypnotism is a big business now. Many doctors, therapists, and dentists use hypnosis to help them in treatment of patients. I had learned early on in my studies of spiritual warfare that blanking of the mind could lead to open doors of demon possession and negative spiritual experiences. I would admonish you to not allow anyone to tamper with your state of mind.

2. Spirit of Error (False Doctrines, Un-submissive, Error, Un-teachable, Defensive/Argumentative, Contentions)

Study to shew thyself approved unto God, a workman that needeth not to be ashamed, rightly dividing the word of truth.But shun profane and vain babblings: for they will increase unto more ungodliness.And their word will eat as doth a canker: 2 Timothy 2:15

Hereby know we the spirit of truth, and the spirit of error 1 John 4:6b

The strongman spirit of error will get you every time if you do not know the Word of God. Ignorance isn't bliss. Even the law holds you accountable for what you do not know. If this strongman is operating in your life, the chances are great that a lying spirit, spirit of heaviness, spirit of haughtiness, familiar spirits, perverse spirit, and spirit of divination is lurking somewhere around.

I thought I was well versed in the scriptures; however, I was dominated by a spirit of error and could not see the error. The mind is so clouded by the strongman, you can't see it. You are absolutely convinced what you believe is true, what your abuser tells you is true, and that everyone else is wrong. Our greatest need is to understand and to be understood. In a verbally abusive relationship, the partner's need to understand and to be understood is not met. The victim in an abusive relationship wants to believe that his or her mate is rational and that understanding can be reached, therefore, he or she will remain in the abusive relationship.

What is a verbally abusive relationship? Verbal abuse is hostile aggression. It is very hard to detect and can be described in terms of experience. Verbal abuse may be overt, such as angry outbursts directed at the partner, or, covert which is hidden by denying knowledge or understanding. Verbal abuse is what Patricia Evans, author of *"The Verbally Abusive Relationship, How to Recognize it and How to Respond"* calls "crazy making". Crazy making was putting it mildly.

In domestic abuse and intimate partner abuse, the victim wants the abuse to stop, and longs for the honeymoon stage. I wanted my family to be happy, healthy, and whole.

These are some experiences I had with the spirit of error:

1. feeling lost, not knowing what to do,
2. disconnected, confused, disoriented,
3. received double messages and would not get a clarification of meaning,
4. feeling bugged by the simple presence of my abuser,
5. searching aimlessly for answers through the Word of God but could not get a handle on what to do,
6. feelings of chaos all the time
7. feeling I wanted to leave but could not, frozen in time warp,
8. not in control of my life,
9. feeling something was wrong but could not pinpoint what was wrong, and
10. I began to hate what I was becoming, not liking myself.

It was not until I began to educate myself about domestic abuse did I realize I was being verbally abused. This type of abuse is also emotionally and psychologically damaging. I was in a vicious cycle and I couldn't stop the spinning. I was no longer submissive as a wife and what I was taught about the duties of a wife. I thought I was fighting back the best way I knew how, and this further exacerbated the situation. The verbal abuse became marital rape. But how can it be marital rape? A wife is supposed to please her husband; you cannot rape your wife. (I must pause to note that a victim is never at fault. No one has the right to usurp the authority or enforce control over another.)

I read the bible over and over trying to find my way out, but the more I read the more confused I became about my predicament. My conservative upbringing and lack of understanding of the bible kept me in bondage. My pride (spirit of haughtiness) would not let me share what was happening to me with anyone. Little did I know my spirit was broken. I walked around as if an albatross was around my neck. I was depressed, oppressed, and stressed beyond measure. I was burdened by my inability to get a grip and pull myself out of the slumps. Everything I did was like animation. I went through the acts of motherhood, but I realized later from my children, what I thought I was doing for them I really wasn't. Victims with children cannot be there emotionally nor psychologically for their children. The nurture and care a child needs in the early stages of their development is hindered because of the psychological and emotional state of the victim. I gave the best love I could give, but it wasn't enough. We were a dysfunctional family in every sense of the word.

I came to understand several risk factors for families where domestic violence and abuse are present.

- Sexual aggression towards wife
- Perpetuation of violence towards children
- Consistent psychopathology
- Increased risk to abuse partner if abused as a child or adolescent
- Girls are high risk to be abused if witnessed parental violence

I also recognized that sexual and power motives were prevalent:

- Intimidation and threats to obtain desired outcomes
- Demeaning comments (Verbal Abuse)
- Monitor and determine partner's activities and associations (Isolation)
- Feelings of powerlessness

All of these factors were truth staring me in the face and I denied them. I was operating under the spirit of error. Verbal abuse in many ways has been built into our socio-cultural living. Our music is demeaning to one another, while television and movies depict graphic abuse of women and children. We live in a society where gender roles foster the belief that male supremacy and stereotypical male and female sex roles cause female subordination, power and control issues.

I am not calling my early Christian teachers false prophets, or false teachers, rather, I like to look at it as a matter of perspective, interpretation, and cultural values about what one believes. Misinterpretation of the scriptures and taking scriptures out of context is the worst form of religious abuse. Using scriptures to keep a victim in an abusive relationship is wrong. Every victim has the right to be safe and to walk in freedom, not bondage. The faith community has to begin dialogue on the dynamics of domestic violence and abuse in their congregations. The myth that dealing with domestic violence and abuse advocates divorce has got to be dispelled. While my specific experience did end in divorce, I can cite many other couples who have worked through their issues and have remained married. Domestic violence and abuse must matter to everyone, from the Pastor to the pew member, and it should matter enough to adopt a perspective and stance of zero tolerance.

The more we allow the lies, myths, and ignorance of domestic violence and abuse to occur, the worst the situation will get. The truth of the Word of God must be able to find its way into the life of victims everywhere. The Word of God is our only true foundation, and will perpetuate truth if the ministers of God rightly divide the Word.

*Brethren, if any of you do err from the truth, and one convert him; Let him know, that he which converteth the sinner from the error of his way shall save a soul from death, and shall hide a multitude of sins. **James 5:19-20***

The perpetrators of domestic violence and abuse must be held accountable and provisions made for their healing and restoration just like the victim. The faith community as God's ambassadors must preach and teach God's grace and hope. God desires every man to walk in the light and knowledge of the truth. I realize the enemy will do anything to keep us from fulfilling our purpose and mission in life. Nevertheless, God's promises and visions are sure. God has given me glimpses and a vision of my purpose.

I will stand upon my watch, and set me upon the tower, and will watch to see what he will say unto me, and what I shall answer when I am reproved. And the Lord answered me, and said, Write the vision, and make it plain upon tables, that he may run that readeth it. For the vision is yet for an appointed time, but at the end it shall speak, and not lie: though it tarry, wait for it; because it will surely come, it will not tarry. **Habakkuk 2:1-3**

I wrote down the vision in my journal and shared it with only a few people. I did this so that when the appointed time came for its fulfillment, they would remember what I had shared with them years ago. I tried on many occasions to push ahead of God to bring the vision to fruition, before its time. Every time I tried, I would become frustrated and felt everyone was holding me back. My error was not trusting God; especially after God had told me on several occasions, "trust and wait". It was not until I had reached my point of breakdown, anxiety, frustration, hurting myself and hurting others, that I realized I had to let go and let God. I thank God that no matter what we try to do, even to our own spiritual demise, God is faithful. At times I thought I was going to lose my mind. I was at a point of what the world would call "compassion fatigue", but in the spirit world, it's called 'a spirit of error'.

We must recognize the sources of stress in our work and relationships. If your work or ministry is helping people who have experienced trauma or crises in their lives, you are particularly vulnerable for compassion fatigue. The more you become aware of the consequences of the ministry or work on an individual and their supporters, the more you realize that you can become burned-out and tired. We must adopt a standard of self care and then be motivated to practice the standards we set.

Let me define a few terms so that you can assess where you are.

1. Burn-out - physically and emotionally exhausted as a result of long term stress.
2. Compassion Stress – derived from experiencing the suffering of others and working to help relieve their stress.
3. Empathic Ability – you are able to comprehend the suffering of others.

4. Empathic Response – communications of compassion of and understanding of another's suffering.
5. Detachment – ability to separate from the suffering and be reminded of what your job or role is.
6. Sense of Satisfaction – Sufferer was helped by your services.
7. Compassion Fatigue – Traumatized by and obsessed with the suffering of others and trying to help them.

In our zeal for ministry, a true heart to worship God, and our desire to fulfill The Great Commandment (Deuteronomy 6:5, Matt. 22:37-38) and The Great Commission (Matt 28:19-20), we sometimes lose our sense of truth. You see, the enemy will mix truth and error and deceive you into believing that you are right and everyone else is wrong. Please realize that the devil knows the Word of God, but will intertwine his lies with the truth. Isn't that what he did in the desert with Jesus? (Luke 4:1-13). This will cause us to do good works, but not God works. You must also remember Satan does not come with anything new, but will repeat his old tricks and lies. The cliché says, 'when God takes us to a new level, we are hindered by a new devil'. But the devil does not have anything new; his tricks are always the same. I had to realize that the enemy was weaving his same web of error in my life. I had gotten to the point of not being submissive, un-teachable, defensive, argumentative, and contentious.

I was so wrapped up in my own pain, my own grief and determination to not allow anyone else to suffer through domestic violence and abuse, that I believed I was obsessed with trying to help other victims. I took on their pain, their suffering, and I still had my own pain to deal with. I didn't understand the term detachment. I didn't realize I had to acquire the ability to separate myself from their suffering, and remember what my role as a victim advocate was about.

Once again the Spirit of God within me knew something was wrong. I didn't like who and what I was becoming. I never stopped praying for God to help me. I never stopped asking God to intervene and show me what was happening to me. My relationships were strained, people would talk about me, but not to me about how I was behaving. I had to do a soul search of myself. It was not pretty, but I recognized that I need- ed to get it together. Whatever I put my hands to do seemed to fall apart. My training engagements, speaking engagements, everything was being cancelled or backfiring. I wasn't getting phone calls returned. I would call meetings and no one would show up. I was mad as hell again. Really, mad at hell.

But God! Somebody say, 'But God!' I was blessed with a trip to get away, rest, and relax. God will take the worst of circumstances and use them for His glory. My time of repentance and solitude turned into the manifestation of the vision God had given me. I attended a church called, The Rock Church. As I sat in the service and the praise and worship was going forth, the vision God had given me came flooding back. What God had called me to do was being revealed right before me. The model of what God wanted me to do was so clear. My heart was so overwhelmed, I could only praise God for His faithfulness. The revealed Word of God, preached in the person of Pastor Lydia, spoke to my spirit.

> *Hearken to me, ye that follow after righteousness, ye that seek the Lord: look unto the rock whence ye are hewn, and to the hole of the pit whence ye are digged. Look unto Abraham your father, and unto Sarah that bare you: for I called him alone, and blessed him, and increased him.* **Isaiah 51:1-2**

I remembered several devotions I had when I was seeking God and praying for my healing from these contentious behaviors. God said that He was calling me back to my priorities, purpose, and values. Pastor Lydia asked us to remember where God had called us from, to remember our salvation call story, and be thankful to God. She said, "Sometimes Jesus will bring people together who would not normally meet or be put together. Sometimes regardless of our nationality we may have to get someone different from us to help us. More times than not, our pride will get in the way of our moving forward in the call of God." The spirit of pride kept me from seeking help during my domestic violence encounters. My pride kept me from reaching out to those who could help me break free and break my silence. So you see, the enemy will keep coming back with the same tricks to deceive us. If we are not careful, the enemy will deceive us to keep us from fulfilling our purpose. We must live a purpose driven life, understanding what God has called us to, and to be on guard always that the enemy will try to prevent us from walking into our destiny.

> *Be sober, be vigilant; because your adversary the devil, as a roaring lion, walketh about, seeking whom he may devour: Whom resist stedfast in the faith, knowing that the same afflictions are accomplished in your brethren that are in the world. But the God of all grace, who hath called us unto his eternal glory by Christ Jesus, after that ye have suffered a while, make you perfect, stablish, strengthen, settle you. 1 Peter 5:8-10*

Sometimes we may not understand in the beginning what God is showing us or telling us through our dreams, however, God has given gifts to His people to interpret dreams just as God did with Joseph and Daniel.

Charles Figley in his book, *The Compassion Fatigue Process*, notes five steps to help you get back in gear: 1) have a commitment to self care, 2) develop strategies for letting go of work or ministry, 3) develop strategies for gaining a sense of achievement, 4) develop strategies for acquiring adequate rest and relaxation, and 5) get and learn to perfect stress reduction methods.[4]

3. Deaf and Dumb Spirit (Crying, Tearing, Children can be harassed. Mental problems, Seizures/Epileptics, Ear problems, Suicidal)

I believe this door was opened through inheritance. There have been on occasion attempts of suicide, depression, seizures, and babies with colic who cried all the time. As I discussed earlier, the harassment that my son experienced with sleep disturbances and nightmares, and my daughters' experiences with seizures, ear infections, and personality disorders is how this spirit manifested in my life. I can only thank God that the attempted suicides in my family were unsuccessful. Nothing is more devastating than having your life and the life of your children destroyed by domestic abuse and violence.

The deaf and dumb spirit can lead one to do dumb things, smoke, drink, experience use of drugs, reckless driving, and many other dumb things which you can probably name that you've done. We see people behaving strangely and doing things contrary to what most people would consider common sense. In domestic violence, there is one myth that people often cite, 'the victim can just leave'. After all, common sense would say, if someone is physically battering you, demeaning you, and controlling you, just leave. Seems pretty dumb to stay, doesn't it?

Satan and other demonic forces are liars.

Ye are of your father the devil, and the lusts of your father ye will do. He was a murderer from the beginning, and abode not in the truth, because there is no truth in him. When he speaketh a lie, he speaketh of his own: for he is a liar, and the father of it. **John 8:44**

Staying in domestic violence and abusive situations can be considered as classical conditioning. The easiest place to start is with a little example. Consider a hungry dog that sees a bowl of food.

Food —-> Salivation

The dog is hungry, the dog sees the food, and the dog salivates. This is a natural sequence of events, an unconscious, uncontrolled, and unlearned relationship. See the food, and then salivate. Now, because we are humans who have an insatiable curiosity, we experiment. When we present the food to the hungry dog (and before the dog salivates), we ring a bell. Thus,

Bell

    with

Food —-> Salivation

We repeat this action (food and bell given simultaneously) at several meals. Every time the dog sees the food, the dog also hears the bell.

Ding-dong = Alpo.

Now, because we are humans with sometimes sick intelligence, we like to play tricks on our pets, so we do another experiment. We ring the bell (Ding-dong), but we don't show any food. What does the dog do?

Bell —-> Salivate

The bell elicits the same response the sight of the food gets. Over repeated trials, the dog has learned to associate the bell with the food and now the bell has the power to produce the same response as the food. (And, of course, after you've tricked your dog into drooling and acting even more stupidly than usual, you must give it a special treat.)

This is the essence of Classical Conditioning. It really is that simple. You start with two things that are already connected with each other (food and salivation). Then you add a third thing (bell) for several trials. Eventually, this third thing may become so strongly associated that it has the power to produce the old behavior.

Now, where do we get the term, "Conditioning" from all this? Let me draw up the diagrams with the official terminology.

Unconditioned —A stimulus (food) and response (saliva) are naturally connected.

"Unconditioned" means that this connection was already present before we got there and started messing around with the dog or the child or the spouse. In domestic violence the connection of family has already been established. I see my daddy; I see my significant other (unconditioned stimulus) and loving feelings are evoked (unconditioned response).

I add a third stimulus (good, bad, ugly, or indifferent)…this is a conditioned stimulus;

I hit you…. I touch you and you're uncomfortable…

I leave you….I reject you…, and loving feelings are evoked (conditioned response), - but something is not right and I don't know what's going on. I am not supposed to have these same loving feelings towards you, but, I can't help myself.

You're conditioned, because now the conditioned stimulus (hit you, kick you, touch you to make you uncomfortable) has taken the place of the unconditioned stimulus(daddy/lover). It still evokes the unconditioned response of having loving feelings toward you. . The strongest application of classical conditioning involves our emotions. Common experience and careful research both confirm that human emotions condition very rapidly and easily. When emotions are intensely felt or have a negative impact, the emotions will condition quickly.

For example, there was a college student who was robbed at gun point by a young man who gave her a choice ("Your body or your life.") It was an unexpected and frightening experience. This event occurred just about dusk and for a long time thereafter, she often experienced moments of dread in the late afternoons particularly when she was just walking around the city. Even though she was quite safe, the lengthening shadows of the day were so strongly associated with the fear she experienced in the rape, that she could not help but feel the emotions over and over again.

Clearly, classical conditioning is a pervasive form of influence in our world. This is true because it is a natural feature of all humans and it is relatively simple and easy to accomplish. Victims of domestic violence and abuse in many ways have been conditioned to the abuse. The oppressor has all the power, the oppressed has no power at all.

Believing that the violence will stop without intervention is deception. Without intervention, the abuse escalates and can end in death. For the perpetrator, the inability to accept what he/she perceived to be rejection of them or their role of dominance over the victim can lead to murder. Walking-out or leaving is also a provoking, intolerable desertion, rejection or abandonment and leads to dumb actions of extreme battering and homicide and/or suicide.

4. Spirit of Infirmity (Arthritis, Oppression, Lingering disorders)

And, behold, there was a woman which had a spirit of infirmity eighteen years, and was bowed together, and could in no wise lift up herself.
Luke 13:11

As we continue to believe in the lies of the enemy and treat our bodies without reverence and respect, we are destined for various diseases and sickness. Our health is negatively affected when we disregard the commandments of God to treat our bodies as living sacrifices, holy and acceptable to God which is our reasonable service (Romans 12:1). We are not living sacrifices for man. Physical, mental, psychological, and emotional abuse is a sin. Assenting or allowing the abuse of our physical, mental, and emotional body is also a sin before God.

I have experienced lingering illnesses, aches and pains in my physical body. I could not understand why I was experiencing problems with my back, my eyes, shoulders, knees, allergies, headaches, and depression. It was not until I understood the dynamics of domestic violence and abuse and spiritual warfare that I gained my healing. I confessed my sin, asked God to reveal any hidden sins, and prayed, binding the spirit of infirmity and loosing the spirit of healing. Never forget that Satan does not go away just because you bind him and cast him out, but will return trying to deceive you and lie to you about the same illnesses from which you have been delivered. He will also try to bring back seven more evil spirits worst than the ones you had before (Luke 11:24-26). As I write this, the deceiver is trying to afflict me with the notion that I have diabetes. But the devil is a liar and I believe God's Word that says, "by Jesus' stripes I am healed." I am doing my part to combat Satan's lies. This means I have to change my diet and living practices. I do not have to take medication, but I would like to give a warning to those of you with serious illnesses, take your medication if a doctor has prescribed it for your healing. Medicine is not a sin. Doctors have been given the knowledge to help fight against sickness and disease. According to your faith, follow what you feel God is leading you to do. Be wise and seek God for wisdom in your medical care (James 1:5) and pray without ceasing (1 Thessalonians 5:17).

There are several things for you to consider if you are in a violent or abusive relationship or have left the relationship but are still experiencing a spirit of infirmity (sickness).

- Make sure you have no un-confessed sin in your life (Psalm 66:18).
- Fear of certain illnesses can open the door to the spirit of infirmity.
- Ignorance or unbelief of the Word of God.
- A breakdown of the body or mind because of abuse, unrealistic work loads, lack of proper rest and nutrition.
- Hereditary weaknesses or diseases that are innocently accepted because of lack of knowledge of his/her rights as a child of God.
- Some people desire to be sick for various illogical reasons.
- People continue to walk in the flesh instead of in the Spirit.[5]

5. Lying Spirit (Lies, False Prophecy, Strong Deception, Accusations)

This manifestation is based on what others have told me. It is very difficult to understand and accept things you don't remember. This is how the enemy can bring strong delusions and deceptions. It was the worst months of my ministry career and ended in my apologizing for something that I do not remember saying or doing. Nevertheless, the enemy will use every opportunity to blind-side us and keep us off balance. One thing we must always remember is to align everything with the Word of God. Satan will take truth and mix the truth with lies, and once that is done there is no longer any truth to what has been spoken or done. My ministry responsibilities became overwhelming due to the lack of respect I felt I was receiving, so I became a complainer. Although my actions were right/truth, my motivation was wrong. It is very difficult to explain, but a lying spirit will make you second guess everything. It will have you justifying things you know are not in line with God's Word. We must guard our hearts during times of testing and trials. Otherwise, we will open ourselves to strong deceptions and lies of the enemies because of our hurts.

The cliché, "hurt people, hurt people", is very much a part of lying spirits. When we hurt we feel justified to hurt others. Sometimes we hurt others not realizing that we are hurting them, but God has called us to a ministry of reconciliation. Jesus gives us transforming initiatives that will combat the lies of the enemy. Satan's lies will say,' retaliate violently and be vengeful by any means necessary'. The truth says, 'turn the other check and go and be reconciled'. Satan's lies will say, 'hate your enemies'. The truth will say,' love your enemies and forgive them'. God's Word gives us power. We have to ask for forgiveness of God and those we have offended because we have believed the lies that the strongman has told us about family, friends, and our brothers and sisters in Christ. We have to evict the thoughts and lies that the enemy tries to plant in our minds concerning our faith, health, and our prosperity. When we believe the strongman's lies, we doubt God and His word as truth. Thank God for the victory over the lying strongman.

6. Familiar Spirits (Peeping and Muttering, Drugs)

A familiar spirit can involve areas surrounding family inheritance. They gain access by any type of mind altering drugs that put the mind in a passive mind state, hallucinations, and/or dreams. The word familiar comes from the root word "family". I can understand this because my family has a history of alcohol and drug abuse. While I have never been able to handle alcohol, I have had experiences with drugs during my teen years.

Drugs have become rampant in our society today. Many lives have been destroyed because of drugs and alcohol. While drugs and alcohol are contributing factors of domestic violence and abuse, they are not the cause. I believe drugs played a significant part in the domestic violence and abuse I experienced within my marriage.

Peeping and muttering is a form of prayer language, however, this form of speaking in tongues sound more like insects clicking and chirping away.[6] Persons using this language would pray under their breath with the sounds of kla, kla, kla, chukka, chukka, chukka, chukka . I have experienced this a couple of times with a very dear friend, however, I have not been able to speak with her concerning these incidents. After all, how do you tell your friend that they may be dealing with satanic influence and the trick of the devil to dupe them into believing they are under the influence of God's Gift of the Spirit?

7 & 8   Spirit of Fear & Spirit of Bondage – (Fears, torment, untrusting, anxiety, stress. Doubts)

My spiritual vitality had been choked right out of me. I was always anxious, not being able to put my finger on what was wrong, but I was constantly in a state of unrest. What I was doing and saying I knew were not aligned with the Word of God. The lying spirits had me bound, justifying and believing the lies that I was right and everybody else was wrong. I thank God for His Word and the Holy Spirit still at work, trying to draw me out of my stupor. A certain scripture continually rang clearly in my ears, " perfect love cast out fear, because fear hath torment" (1 John 4:18). If I was right, why was I feeling so tormented about my relationships? Why was I so torn about my friendships and family relationships? It was difficult to have joy and it seemed impossible to love people who I felt were against me.

God did not give us a spirit of fear (2 Timothy 1:7). I began to doubt myself. I doubted whether or not I truly understood the Word. I started to question whether or not the Word was the truth, and if what I believed was wrong. I was no longer confident about my abilities. I felt like I was tied in knots and there was no way out. How I was dealing with my children and family members was spinning out of control. Thank God for His faithfulness. I later found out I had people praying for me. When we can't pray for ourselves, it is wonderful to know that the body of Christ is praying for you. The song, "Somebody prayed for me, had me on their mind. Took the time to pray for me. I'm so glad they prayed for me." There has never been a song so true and I am so grateful.

9. & 11. Perverse Spirit/ Spirit of Whoredom – (Broken spirit, Abortion, Child Abuse, Incest, Contentious/Chronic Dissatisfaction, Fornication, Unfaithfulness/Adultery)

God created man and woman, husband and wife to live in harmony one with another. He said be fruitful and multiply. God created and ordained the first family. The twisted mind of a perverse man or woman is a stronghold. Sexual promiscuousness started at a young age. Playing house as mentioned before opened the door of sexual perversion. Fornication, losing my virginity before I was married also gave Satan access into my life. Later having an abortion because of a date rape only compounded the problem and allowed the spirit of perversion to embed itself deeper in my life. This stronghold opened the door for even more perversion, marital rape, incest, and a contentious spirit. When we expose ourselves or align ourselves with others who have strongholds in their lives, the sexual union joins you together, '…and they become one flesh' (Ephesians 5:31)), and you can take on their demons. I found myself always at a debate with my abuser. He said left, and I would say right. He would say go, and I would stop. I could not and would not agree with much of anything he had to say. I had lost all respect for him and for myself. I didn't like him and I didn't like what I was becoming. I knew I was right and everything about him was wrong.

I was totally out of synch with God's universe. God created the universe in order, but I was in utter chaos. I felt like I was living outside my body. Nothing could possibly be real. All this had to be a bad dream and one day I would wake up and everything would be fine. As you can see, early childhood experiences can impact your life later on down the road.

What we do and decisions we make in our teen years can have far reaching implications that can damage our lives when we are older. I only wish I had listened to my parent's wisdom.

10. Spirit of Jealousy – (Anger-Rage, Revenge-Spite, Envy, Jealousy, Strife)

I was sure my husband was having extra-marital affairs, but I couldn't prove it. Although I enjoyed when he was gone, I couldn't help but feel he was cheating on me. I experienced the conditioning of the love-hate relationship and that drove me to the anger and rage. I couldn't understand how I could love a person that emotionally and then have him sexually abuse me. The longer I stayed in the relationship the seeds of anger, spite, envy, and jealousy grew. If these seeds are allowed to fester and grow, they will only grow bigger and bigger and the roots of them will sink deeper and deeper. These roots can grow so deep you don't recognize the bondage you are in. Only the supernatural power of God can set you free.

I became envious of my friends, family members, and even some members of my church family. I began to work towards gaining the highest level of management in my job. I was on the fast track to upward mobility at work. I thought if I could gain prestige and status on my job, I would feel better about myself. It was only the abuse I was experiencing at home that pushed me to extreme measures of envy and strife in other areas of my life. I was too proud to ask for help and suffered in silence.

After all, this was how it was in families. "Wives be submissive to your husbands. Wives are to reverence their husbands." I thought everyone's marriage but mine was made in heaven. What I didn't realize was that like I faked joy in the presence of outsiders, so do others who experience the trauma of domestic violence and abuse.

13. Spirit of Haughtiness – (Arrogant, Pride, Self-Deception, Rebellion. Strife, Contentious)

I really didn't see myself as prideful. I thought I was giving God all the credit for my success, my material prosperity, and family life. I thought I was being the obedient wife, but I was fighting for my life. I didn't realize that trying to hold onto my sanity was because of a prideful spirit. I could handle it. I thought I was giving it to God, but in reality, I was finding coping mechanisms that did not honor God at all. The deception in most cases like mine, is that a person appearing to have much success on the outside, if you dig deep enough underneath the outside glitter and glamour, there is usually brokenness, drug or health problems, broken relationships, extreme unhappiness, and loneliness. I rebelled against my abuser, and that opened another door to the spirit of rebellion. Oh, the tangle web we weave when we refuse to respond and leave abusive relationships.

Failure to act upon the abuse, I was sinning against God and against my body.

> *What know ye not that your body is the temple of the Holy Ghost, which*
> *ye have in you, and ye have of God and you are not your own. But*
> *you've been brought with a price. Therefore glorify God in your body*
> *and in your spirit, which are God's.* ***1 Corinthians 6:19-2***

Domestic violence and abuse defames the body and spirit of humanity. If you are in a domestic violence or abusive relationship and you find yourself prideful, arrogant, contentious, scornful, anger (against children, abuser), obstinate, stubborn, rebellious, and boastful, please take a spiritual break and check your spirit. If you see these things manifesting themselves, get out. Take immediate actions necessary to get them out of your life or get the person who is contributing to this behavior out of your life. We must humble ourselves, admit to God we cannot do it alone, and seek God and spiritual counselors to help us move to healing and wholeness.

12. Spirit of Heaviness – (Excessive Mourning, Sorrow-Grief, Insomnia, Broken-Heart, Self-Pity, Rejection, Despair-Dejection-Hopelessness, Depression, Suicidal Thoughts, Inner Hurts-Torn Spirit, Heaviness)

Can I get an amen, somebody? The spirit of heaviness just about sums up the results of victims living with domestic violence and abuse. A family torn apart, the joy of living and family life have been destroyed.

We are in a perpetual state of grief and sorrow.

It is natural to go through a state of mourning, sorrow, and grief in the loss of something valuable and/or treasured. It takes time for us to recover and adjust both physically and psychologically to the changes we must face. We realize that grief is a God given emotion, but God does not expect us to continue long in our grieving. Suffering in domestic violence and abuse is like grieving, but the grieving is not the loss of a loved one through death, but the loss of love, the death of dreams and a future that you thought would be different. It is the death of a promise, the loss of potential, the broken heart that you gave, expecting it to be cared for, cherished and loved until death you would part. It's living through rejection and despair. It's fighting to get up everyday and face a world you feel has turned its back on you. It's combating suicidal thoughts that say, it's better to die than to keep living like this. It's waking up to morning and rather than saying, "Good morning God", you say, "Good God it's morning!"

Dreading what the day will bring. Inner hurts so deep, you can't breathe. The promises and vows made to unite you as one, now tearing your spirit and soul apart. When all these things are dying around you, it will breed fear. Death magnified creates fear. Fear of the unknown. Fear of not knowing if you will live to see the day end. Fear that your children will be alright. Fear of what will happen today to warrent my abuse. Then the fear turns to self-pity. We pity ourselves because we have become immobilized. We cannot act, we cannot leave. Why did God leave me alone to deal with this, to cope with this abuse alone? Why is there no help for me? Self-pity leads to loneliness. We are all alone and no one knows nor understands what I am going through. So we retreat into a shell. We give up and think we are destined to be abused for the rest of our lives. Many times because of verbal abuse, we come to believe what our abuser tells us because that is the only voice we hear, day in and day out.

The relationship is broken, our marriage is a disaster and we get depressed, but we know that God is our refuge; a very present help in the time of trouble. When we have reached this stage of heaviness, we are in

Notes

[1] www.encyclopdia.laborlawtalk.com

[2] The Psychology of Blacks, pp. 105

[3] Strongman's His Name, pp. 15-23

[4] Figley, 1995;2002

[5] Strongman's His Name, p. 84

[6] Strongman's His Name, p. 31

trouble. It is during these times that the heaviness is too hard for us to bear alone, and only God can pull us up and out.

1. Spirit of Divination

2. Spirit of Error

3. Deaf and Dumb Spirit

4. Spirit of Infirmity

5. Lying Spirit

6. Familiar Spirits

7. Spirit of Bondage

8. Spirit of Fear

9. Perverse Spirit

10. Spirit of Jealousy

11. Spirit of Whoredom

12. Spirit of Heaviness

13. Spirit of Haughtiness

Chapter 9

"THE NAME OF JESUS AND THE SIGNIFICANCE OF THE BLOOD"

My little children, these things write I unto you, that ye sin not. And if any man sin, we have an advocate with the Father, Jesus Christ the righteous: And he is the propitiation for our sins: and not for ours only, but also for the sins of the whole world. ***1 John 2:1-2***

Thank God we have an advocate, Jesus Christ, who is for us and more than a world against us. When we think of an advocate, we realize we have someone who is a supporter, a backer, a promoter, a believer, an activist, a campaigner, and a sponsor. Wow! Who would not want an advocate that is there to push and cheer you on. One who will believe in you and fight for you. One who will champion your cause and your welfare, always looking out for your best interests. Jesus will fight for you. Jesus has already won the battle.

And all this assembly shall know that the Lord saveth not with sword and spear: for the battle is the Lord's, and he will give you (the enemy) into our hands. ***I Samuel 17:47***

Isn't it interesting that Jesus went into the wilderness full of the Holy Ghost, *And Jesus being full of the Holy Ghost returned from Jordan, and was led by the Spirit into the wilderness, (Luke 4:1),* and thirteen (13) verses later, *And Jesus returned in the power of the Spirit into Galilee: and there went out a fame of him through all the region round about;* he came out with the power of the Holy Ghost. In case you didn't catch it, our number thirteen. I identified 13 spirits that were oppressing me. Our destiny cannot be destroyed. Your road to deliverance will come through the things that have tried to destroy you. But God has already made the provision through Jesus Christ. The finished work of Jesus sealed our victory. We are seated in heavenly places with Jesus, high above all the things that come against us. We have been given power and authority over all devils, and to cure diseases (Luke 9:1). Jesus said, *"Behold, I give unto you power to tread on serpents and scorpions, and over all the power of the enemy: and nothing shall by any means hurt you (Luke 10:19)".* Satan is trying to talk you into a fight that's already been won? He wanted me to fight all the forces that came against me. I had to ask myself, "Why and how can I fight a battle that has already been fought and won?". Stay focused and do not be distracted by the trauma and tragedies of life. Stop living beneath your privileges. Your blessing is coming through your disfigurement and your pain. Remember who you are and what God has done in your life in the past. Your past has been changed. You are in control. "God has not given you the spirit of fear, but of power, love, and a sound mind" **2 Timothy 1:7**.

With more power and authority than the Thirteenth Amendment of the U.S. Constitution and Congress, the Word of God declares, we will not be slaves nor involuntarily serve in the enemy's camp. We are empowered to enforce the Word of God. We are no longer slaves in forced labor. Satan tries to enslave us through lies, tricks, and deceit. He goes about as a roaring lion seeking whom he may devour. The law of sin kills. Sin entered into the world when Adam and Eve disobeyed God. Their disobedience caused their spiritual death. Romans 6:23 says, *the wages of sin is death, but the gift of God is eternal life through Jesus Christ our Lord.* Thanks be to God, *but God commendeth his love toward us, in that, while we were yet sinners, Christ died for us (Romans 5:8).* Jesus paid the ultimate price for your sin and mine. Because Jesus satisfied the penalty for sin, we don't have to die. Domestic violence and abuse kills. Women and children have died under the hands of their abusers. Women have been disfigured, stalked, kidnapped, and beaten almost to death. Why do we stay and be enslaved to our abuser? We have the name of Jesus as our authority to bind the spirits that keep us in bondage. *Verily I say unto you, Whatsoever ye shall bind on earth shall be bound in heaven: and whatsoever ye shall loose on earth shall be loosed in heaven. Again I say unto you, That if two* *of you shall agree on earth as touching any thing that they shall ask, it shall be done for them of my Father which is in heaven. For where two or three are gathered together **in my name**, there am I in the midst of them.* (Matthew 18:18-20) Whatever we need, we ask in the name of Jesus. *The name of the Lord is a strong tower: the righteous runneth into it, and is safe (Proverbs 18:10).* When we cry out to God for help, God will hear us, *"for thou hast been a shelter for me, and a strong tower from the enemy (Psalm 61:3)."*

The blood of Jesus made the atonement for our sin. The blood of Jesus has power and covers the sin and sins in our lives. The love of Jesus covers a multitude of sin. Jesus' blood was shed for the remission of sin. Knowing, without the shedding of blood, there is no remission for sin (Hebrews 9:22-28). The blood of Jesus is against all the powers that Satan has tried to enact in our lives. The blood of Jesus covers our families, our children, our job, our homes, and every place our feet shall tread. We are justified (cleared of guilt) by His blood (Romans 5:9); we have redemption (exchanged His life for ours) through His blood (Ephesians 1:7); and we overcome (victorious) by the blood of the Lamb (Revelation 12:19).

Jesus entered into a world where violence was at every hand, a world in which people were victimized over and over again. Today, our world has not changed: the poor is neglected, governments are corrupt, unemployment is high, women are being beaten and raped by military forces, children are abducted, abused and killed, HIV/AIDS is killing masses of people, and the earth is being plundered of its natural resources and our society and world perpetuates violence at home and across the seas.

Jesus entered our world to clash with the normalcy of violence, and a world built on hostility, especially towards women, children, the poor, the marginalized, and the oppressed. Jesus lived, died, and was resurrected to become the chief cornerstone of a new humanity that would no longer promote violence and live at the expense of victims. The blood of Jesus on that old rugged cross exposed our world to the violence that it is, and showed us a more perfect way through love, God's love, which is greater than our murderous passions and desire for power and control of our world and others. God's glory can and does shine even in the deepest night of human savagery; He wishes all would be saved and come to repentance.[1] His shed blood allowed us the opportunity for freedom. If you are in a domestic violence or intimate partner violence relationship, God wants you to be free. The price for your freedom has already been paid. Walk in it!

Notes

[1] Faith Seeking Understanding, pp. 158-159

Chapter 10

"MAKING PEACE WITH YOUR PAST"

Peace I leave with you, my peace I give unto you: not as the world giveth, give I unto you. Let not your heart be troubled, neither let it be afraid **John 14:27**

Be careful for nothing; but in every thing by prayer and supplication with thanksgiving let your requests be made known unto God. And the peace of God, which passeth all understanding, shall keep your hearts and minds through Christ Jesus. **Philippians 4:6-7**

My Prayer before God

My soul is poured out like water. Morning and night I awake with fear and trembling. I cry out to the Lord to help me and my cries seem to go up like smoke. I awake at night and my mind is vexed and in terror. The enemy oppresses me all the day long and I cannot find a hiding place. I call to God, "O Lord, help me!" But there is no help. I am in a dry and barren place. I say, "When will deliverance come? When will God spare me and build my soul once again?"

I awake and I saturate my mind with the Word of God. I listen day and night, yet peace seems to be far from me. My head hurts day and night and comfort eludes me. "Where are you, O God? Is this my punishment for my sins? Have my transgressions found me out? Have mercy on me, O God. Deliver me from the oppression of my enemies." My soul, my soul is in a dry and barren land. I need water to quench my thirst. I long for your refreshing. I need your rivers of living water to purify and satisfy my longings. I wait for you, O Lord. For none other can save me nor deliver me. Only you, O God, are my refuge. Though I am slain all the day long, I will trust and wait.

God's Answer

Out of the depths have I cried unto thee, O Lord. Lord, hear my voice:

let thine ears be attentive to the voice of my supplications. If thou, Lord, shouldest mark iniquities, O Lord, who shall stand? But there is forgiveness with thee, that thou mayest be feared. I wait for the Lord, my soul doth wait, and in his word do I hope. My soul waiteth for the Lord more than they that watch for the morning: I say, more than they that watch for the morning.

Let Israel hope in the Lord: for with the Lord there is mercy, and with him is plenteous redemption. And he shall redeem Israel from all his iniquities. **Psalm 130**

The Spirit of the Lord led me to this Psalm that morning. Those of you whose mornings and nights are dark and tumultuous and you long for and trust that morning will come, so you must resolve within yourself, "I will trust and wait for God to deliver me from the pain and sorrow of domestic violence and abuse. I will trust and wait for God all the day long, no matter how long it takes. More than they who watch for the morning, do I wait on you, O God."

God's Provision for our Peace

Jesus is the provision for us to have peace with God. The trusted work that Jesus died at the cross is the complete atonement of our sin and the forgiveness we have with God. Our salvation past was secured when Jesus died and the penalty for sin was paid and satisfied. When Jesus sent the Holy Spirit to be our comforter and guide, our salvation present (everyday) is secure because we have power over sin. Sin is no longer our master. When Jesus returns, our salvation future, the very presence of sin will be abolished forever.

Making Peace with My Past

Facing the abuse and violence of my childhood came flooding back to my memory as I searched my soul to understand why I was not at peace. I remembered a family member's abuse (I was able to finally confront them as an adult as a result of dealing with it in my own counseling sessions). They explained to me that another family member had introduced them to sex. I remembered my father's drinking and fighting with my mother. I remembered playing house with my siblings, and naturally, if you are playing house there is a mommy and a daddy. Never underestimate the power of television and what children see. What children see, they imitate. Mommies and daddies have sex, so we imitate them. I remembered family members rubbing up against me and making my body feel good. I remembered exploring my own body as a child and as I got older. I remember losing my virginity at the age of sixteen and having sex with different men until finally one became my husband and abuser. By the way, I must not forget one of the men date-raped me and I got pregnant. I remembered having an abortion as a result of the date rape. I remembered the abortion after having my first child during my marriage. I remembered the pain and abuse of my marriage. I remembered the abuse of my children. I remembered the struggle and the hurt of the divorce. I remember the alienation from my family because they just didn't understand. I remembered the unhealthy relationships I continued to get entangled with.

I remembered the struggle of my children trying to survive the abuse and to live normal lives. I remembered the pain that I saw in my son's eyes as he lived with the truth of his father's actions. I remembered the agony and turmoil of trying to reconcile my beliefs and values with the reality of the man I married. The man who was supposed to love, honor and cherish me, was abusive. I remembered struggling to make ends meet because my abuser refused to give financial support for his three children. I remembered only wanting to wake up to realize this was a terrible nightmare.

My soul, my soul, O' my soul...why can't I find peace? The war of my memories were taking me into captivity. Where could I find rest from the thoughts that plagued my mind?

> *Come unto me, all ye that labour and are heavy laden, and I will give you rest. Take my yoke upon you, and learn of me; for I am meek and lowly in heart: and ye shall find rest unto your souls. For my yoke is easy, and my burden is light.* **Matthew 11:28-30**

Oh, if I had wings of an eagle, I would fly away and be at rest. Rest and peace only comes with reconciling your past and casting forth the spiritual forces (evil, Satan) that have bound you and loosing the spiritual forces (good, God) that will bring you peace. Making peace with my past required me to denounce and bind all the demonic forces and spirits from the many men to whom my body had been joined. I had to bind and cast out all the evil spirits that were oppressing me as a result of the choices I had made and the doors I had opened that gave the enemy a toehold to have entrance into my life. Again, knowingly or unknowingly, willingly or unwillingly, any doors to give the enemy entrance into your life still yields the same results. I had to close doors that had been opened through generational curses (choices) that I have seen through at least six generations (teenage pregnancy and unwed mothers). Simple choices we make, and decisions we make have far reaching implications. If you know and understand the doors you have opened that gave Satan access into your life, you would be careful to make better choices and wiser decisions, because they would be God choices and decisions. What we do at sixteen, even our early childhood years can determine who and what we become at 25, 35, and even 50 years old.

I had to ask God's forgiveness for my own sins first and then for the bad choices I had made. I had to ask God to forgive the sins of my forefathers and mothers. I had to thank God for the provision, Jesus Christ that freed me from the penalty of sin, that has given me power over sin, and the faith to believe that one day the very presence of sin would be abolished. I had to thank God that I had the authority over the enemy and all his demonic forces. And then I had to exercise that authority by speaking the Word, binding the demonic forces, and casting them out.

*Then he called his twelve disciples together, and gave them power and authority over all devils, and to cure diseases. **Luke 9:1***

*Verily I say unto you, Whatsoever ye shall bind on earth shall be bound in heaven: and whatsoever ye shall loose on earth shall be loosed in heaven. **Matthew 18:18***

Loosing the Spirit of God in my life through the Word of God was my answer to survival, restoration, and peace. I began to immerse myself in the Word. I listened to the bible on tapes at night with headphones. I read and I studied the Word. I meditated on the Word and listened to the Word being preached and took notes. Any way I could get the Word in my heart and in my hand, I did it. I then had to pray constantly in season and out of season.

*Pray without ceasing. **1 Thessalonians 5:17***

Spiritual warfare is not praying, but praying is a central offensive weapon in warfare.

*Praying always with all prayer and supplication in the Spirit, and watching thereunto with all perseverance and supplication for all saints; **Ephesians 6:18***

The opposite of war is peace, and we must do everything to make peace. The enemy of your soul wants to make war on you, but God has called us to peace and reconciliation. The memories of the past can cause

> *Serenity Prayer*
>
> *God grant me the SERENITY to accept the things I cannot change,*
>
> *COURAGE to change the things I can,*
>
> *And the WISDOM to know the difference.*

you unrest, struggle, and depression. Make peace with your past, because you cannot change it.

Facing the pain of your past with God's help can bring you the rest for your weary soul that you are searching and longing to have. Let God be true and every man a liar. God has promised us peace. You will only find that peace in the Word of God and through a relationship with God's son, Jesus Christ. Make peace with your past and then make peace with one another. Allowing God's peace to calm your soul will enable you to live out your purpose in life without distractions and to focus on the things that God has called you to do.

Thou wilt keep him in perfect peace, whose mind is stayed on thee: because he trusteth in thee. Trust ye in the Lord for ever: for in the Lord JEHOVAH is everlasting strength: **Isaiah 26:3-4**

God I thank you for your peace. Let your peace abide with me always.

Finally, brethren, whatsoever things are true, whatsoever things are honest, whatsoever things are just, whatsoever things are pure, whatso-

ever things are lovely, whatsoever things are of good report; if there be any virtue, and if there be any praise, think on these things.

Those things, which ye have both learned, and received, and heard, and seen in me, do: and the God of peace shall be with you. ***Philippians 4:8-9***

Your journey to finding peace is ongoing. This letter was written in February, 2000. This was a letter that started my journey to making peace with my past. I also want to share with you excerpts from my journal as I began my healing and restoration to wholeness and peace with God. It was then I discovered my God ordained purpose for life and the unique mission that God had called me to fulfill.

We each have a purpose in life. Even in our disobedience of doing our own thing, our own way, and in our own time; God can take our trials and disobedience and work them to His glory. The story of Job is also a testament of Satan's desire to try us, attack us, and wreak havoc in our lives. But remember the key is, Satan has to get permission from God to do anything to us (Job 1:1-12). God allows things to come in our lives in addition to what we bring on ourselves as a result of our freewill choices and decisions.

A Letter from Jesus (written February 6, 2000)

Dear Maxine,

Why didn't you come out today when I called for you? I know you have a lot to hide because I know what we have gone through. There are so many things I don't understand either. However, in order to understand where we are now, we must revisit where we have been. I know that God does not allow us to go through anything that we cannot conquer and use for His glory. We have stood by the sidelines in so many things and allowed them to happen to us. But it is time now to take charge and know exactly who it is God originally created us to be. Not what the enemy has put forth or blocked out. We must together realize that God has a greater purpose for us and the hindrances to our ultimate destiny must be removed.

We are so fearful of what others will say about us because they have labeled us and we have conformed to their image. But God has a greater good of who He says we are. Please do not hide from me. Together let us discover what God created us to be. Let us live out the rest of our lives not fearful of man, but fearful of not knowing who God says we really are. Won't you please take this journey with me? I am afraid also because I do not know what I will discover. But I am willing to try. I am willing to I cannot even say it. The very thought of exposing who I am brings me great anxiety and fear. No wonder you will not come out. But if we try together, we can make it.

(Journal Excerpt)

March 6, 2000

Read: Matthew 14:28-33

Title: A Leap of Faith

God calls us to a life of trust and belief in Him. When we first came into the knowledge of God, He guided us and taught us through simple object lessons. His love surrounded us and the trials and troubles we went through we always felt His presence right there to carry us through. God fed us the milk of His word; and like the calcium in milk that helps our bones grow, thicken and become strong, the milk of the Word was suf-ficient enough to sustain us and help us grow in our faith.

As we begin to develop as children, our parents give us food with a little more substance. This food required us to exercise our jaw muscles and teeth to change the consistency of the food so that it could be swal-lowed and digested. So the Word came to us that required us to exercise our faith and grow a little more to understand the things of God.

Jesus called his disciples at a time in their lives when they were like babes, unable to feed on the things of substance in God's Word. Jesus *taught them, corrected them, and showed them the way of life. Each experience and each lesson was an opportunity for them to grow deeper and deeper in their faith and relationship with Him. Jesus called them first to be <u>taught by Him</u> and then to <u>learn of Him</u>. Then He gave them tasks that required <u>willingness and obedience</u>. One of those tasks was to follow Him.*

Eventually, Jesus gave them tasks that took more faith to complete and more obedience to grow.

One day Jesus called Peter to take a <u>"Leap of Faith"</u> by walking on the water. Our finite minds know the laws of gravity that implies it is impossible to walk on water. So too, God calls us to a work that we know in our finite minds we cannot complete because we don't have the knowledge, the finances, and the resources. We don't have the strength, nor the ability, nor do we have the hope to complete such tasks. We think it is impossible to complete.

Peter was willing and obedient to the call of Jesus to "come". Peter stepped out on the water, not doubting and not fearful that he could accomplish the Lord's command that bid him to come. As long as Peter kept his eyes on Jesus, he was able to do the impossible. However, when he began to look around and see all the reasons of why this task could not be done, he began to doubt, he began to waver, Peter began to sink.

We have to be willing and obedient to take that first step, that "leap of faith" that will help us to do the impossible. Then we must keep our focus on Jesus and not turn our eyes away from Him. Trust God and do not doubt that He will help you to do the impossible.

Faith in God and the promises God have given you in the Bible are tantamount to your healing and restoration. Overcoming Satan and the demonic forces he has set up in the world and in your life through domestic violence cannot be won by spineless, jelly back Christians who do not and cannot fight to tear down the strongholds and fortresses that have been setup in their lives and the world.

Chapter 11

"HIS STORY"

The Abuser's Story and Commentary

By Harold Dean Trulear, Ph.D.

Can a man who is a perpetrator of abuse be redeemed?

The answer to this question requires a complete, deliberate approach. Ultimately, the answer is "yes," for with God, all things are possible. We know that the "whosoever" in that marvelous text "For God so loved the world that He gave His only begotten Son that whosoever believeth in Him should not perish but have everlasting life" comes without exception or qualification. The challenge of the redemption of the man who perpetrates abuse requires that we dig deeply into the notion of redemption and its implications for our ministry to men who abuse their families. I know, for not only have I dealt with this issue as a pastor, teacher and evangelist, God had to take me through a series of experiences to deliver me from my own abusive behavior.

While redemption is possible, and reconciliation between one who abuses and the one who has been abused is the highest good that can be sought, for such to occur requires an understanding of redemption as a process and a prioritizing of steps toward redemption, healing and reconciliation. One of the reasons that this chapter appears so late in this book is because the first priority of ministry to women who are abused is their safety. There can be no reconciliation- indeed no hope for redemption for the one who abuses, unless the abuse stops. Domestic violence is wrong. It is sin and must be dealt with in a fashion that takes its evilness seriously. Even when Jesus showed mercy to the women caught in adultery, he punctuated their encounter saying "Go and sin no more."

This evil is rooted in our depraved nature- our separation from God. Evil is reinforced through the work of Satan, how he attacks individual lives, and how he presides over the principalities and powers that oversee society and institutionalize evil. That is why we have approached this subject with an understanding of evil that takes seriously both individual behavior and the lies society and its institutions (including the church) tell women about their abuse. The one who comes to "kill, rob and destroy" delights in seeing violence in the home and has developed both individual and corporate strategies for it to occur- even amongst church people. If perpetrators of domestic violence are to be redeemed, we must confront their behavior in all its evil, and the first step in this redemptive process is to get the violence to stop.

There are three ways for domestic violence to stop: separation, death, or reconciliation. Too often, the church, in its effort to seek reconcilia-tion, avoids the first separation, and the result is continued violence or death. The woman's safety is the first priority, even if our goal is redemp-tion and possible reconciliation. That is why we have not even introduced this question of the redemption of the man who abuses until now. We did not want the concerned reader to rush to reconciliation without a clear understanding of the evil nature of abuse, the terrible hurt inflicted by abuse, and the awful consequences of an inadequate response by the peo-ple of God.

For this reason, we have pressed the notion that the abuse must stop, and the only way to ensure this is to separate the one who abuses from the one who is abused. This separation also helps the abuser. The man who abuses obviously has difficulty with his situation and needs a new or different environment in order for him to focus on himself and his need for change. If there is something about his relationship with his wife and/or children that triggers his behavior, removal from the situation affords him the opportunity to come to terms with his behavior and be changed. Notice I did not say something about his wife's behavior, rather something about the relationship. Too long we have talked to abused women and asked them about how their behavior triggers the violence, and sought to have them change their behavior so that the husband will

not become violent. This approach blames the victim for her own suffering, and also blocks the way for the man who abuses to receive the healing he needs to change. And change he must, because his behavior is
wrong, sinful, evil, and contrary to the purposes of God. Helping the
woman to change so she won't trigger his behavior actually impedes any
hope for the change of the relationship- true reconciliation.

If there is something about the relationship that needs to change (not
the woman's behavior) then we are in a position to focus on what the
abuser brings to the relationship as a person- and deal with what goes on
inside this man that makes him violent. This is what must change for the
man who abuses to be redeemed! He must undergo a total transformation. This is the nature of redemption.

The movie, 'Love Story', gave us the now well worn line "Love
means never having to say you're sorry." The reality of domestic violence demonstrates that abuse means saying you're sorry over and over
again, but seeing little if any change. Almost all men who abuse, when
they come to a moment of sanity, say they are sorry. Many cry, beg,
plead, and even offer a well intentioned change of behavior for a season.
Some offer flowers, dinner, a vacation, and a renewal of dating behavior,
any of a number of things that are intended to say they have changed. But
have they? Or in my case, did I?

I always said I was sorry, and I meant it. What I did not realize was that sorry was not enough- sorry did not mean I've changed, it simply meant that I deeply regretted what had happened. To regret an action and to be transformed so that the action will not occur again are two different things. As church leaders, we all have met people who were rueful concerning their behavior with NO intention of changing, or at the least, no idea of how to change. And simply giving one's life to Christ is no guarantee that a particular behavior will change thoroughly and permanently. If that were the case, the word "backslider" would not be in our vocabulary. But just as we know that the process of spiritual growth is necessary for the believer to win victory over sin in one's life, the transformation of the one who abuses requires attention to process, discipline and growth. It starts with helping the abuser to understand himself, for God wants him to be transformed. God wants him to be redeemed. In short, God calls the abuser to repentance.

Repentance goes far beyond saying "I'm sorry." Even a heartfelt "I'm sorry" falls short of the biblical ideal of repentance. Repentance translates the Greek word "metanoia" which means a "total turning." It describes not just an attitude of regret, but a change of behavior. When John the Baptist declared that people should "Repent and be baptized," he was not simply asking them to say they were sorry. He was calling them to a new and changed life. Jesus' call to "Repent" points to the "kingdom of God at hand" and challenges the hearer to believe the gospel. The gospel- the good news- says that you do not have to live this way any more. The good news for the abuser is that you don't have to be violent any more. God can set you free from your violent tendencies and behaviors.

The abuser is a person, too, one in need of radical change in his life. The abuser is someone God loves, Christ died for and the Spirit yearns to indwell and lead. The abuser is a troubled soul- the poster child for the adage "hurt people hurt people." The abuser can be redeemed, indeed God desires the redemption of the abuser, and for that to happen, the abuser must first be put in a situation where he can no longer abuse any-one so that his focus can be on his own behavior, not the others he believes triggers his behavior.

I was angry with my wife. She did things that pushed my buttons, triggered a rage of which I had no idea was possible. After all, I was raised in a Christian home, went to church every Sunday, professed Christ as a child and never saw violence in my home. I had answered the call to preach, been trained in religious studies, theology and ministry, received ordination and worked in a local church. I was angry with my wife- what I did not know was that I was angry before I met her- and that while my focus was on "changing her so she wouldn't make me mad," what needed to change was me.

Perhaps you are stuck on my testimony right now. You may be saying that if I was an abusive husband that I couldn't have been truly saved. I think I was, God truly knows, and without discernment, anybody else is guessing. I believe that there are men who have been saved, know God (though they struggle with their relationship with him) and perpetrate acts of violence. They are truly sorry, mean it when they apologize and say it will never happen again, and then- because they never allow God to dig deeply into their hearts and show them the root of their behavior- they eventually repeat the same. But redemption is still possible.

You may be surprised to hear me say I am an ordained minister. Do not be, rather mourn the fact that in most accountings of reports of domestic violence, clergy are in the top three professions along with physicians and law enforcement officers. All three professions share high levels of stress and low levels of recognition. All three professions share a commitment to caring and a sense of under appreciation for that caring. All three professions share a sense of loneliness that "no one really understands what I go through," that dulls the mind and wounds the soul. Still, these are not excuses for violent behavior, for we all know persons in these professions who are not abusers. Rather, they point us to the fact that there are stress related factors to certain professions that exacerbate some already present tendencies toward abuse and domestic violence. Satan both uses his influence in the personal life of an individual and his organized schemes that control patterns of behavior (principalities and powers) to bring about his desired effects of violence.

Neither does this mean we should expect or excuse people in these professions. Violence against women is wrong. Any man can be an abuser, just as any man can be an alcoholic. There is no guaranteed profile and it does not appear on the resume. What many abusers do have in common is a deep anger that has festered for years. It is a deep anger that manifests itself as rage and begets the form of violence we have discussed in earlier sections of this book.

Some have said that what abusers have in common is an experience of abuse themselves as a child. They point to this not only to help us pay more attention to child abuse and its consequences, but also so that we can be prepared to help abusers get beyond their abusive behavior. I point to anger rather than a history of abuse as the common root of abusive behavior for two reasons. First, not all persons who have been abused become abusers. Second, there are abusers who have no history of abuse. It is unscriptural to point to one's past experiences as the primary cause of current behavior. In social sciences we call that "behavioral determinism." It says that we are simply the sum product of what has happened to us. The Bible rejects such a notion. It points to our root creation in the image of God, fallenness through Adam's sin, and hope for change through Jesus Christ. The "light which lighteth every man which is come into the world" shows us that we are more than the sum of our experiences. God has given us the capacity to choose- a reflection of being created in the image of a God who chooses. So while we are clearly heavily influenced by our past history and experiences, we are never bound and determined by them. Understanding them, however, and the anger to rage to violence progression many of us have found ourselves in, is part of the healing process that leads to redemption and reconciliation.

Rage is anger out of control. Anger by itself is not sin. Anger is part of our created being- in the image of God, for even God gets angry. Anger is a gift from God designed to motivate us to destroy that which is harmful, but God never intended anger to rage out of control. The Scripture says to "be angry and sin not; do not let the sun go down on your anger." Anger should motivate, but never control. It puts us in touch with an extreme dislike of something, a need to resist, even fight something. Our real fight as believers is against Satan, but there are men whose anger becomes uncontrollably directed against another human being- even a loved one. I was one.

Many abusers suffer from what has been called a "silent rage." To be sure, rage can erupt in an emotional outburst that almost seems to come from somewhere other than the person himself. In other settings, the man who abuses has exhibited good tendencies and behaviors, but this rage- this uncontrolled anger- can seem at odds with the individual's behavior in other settings. Some abusers appear to be still waters running deep, but with churning eddy far beneath the surface.

There is a different silence than the appearance of calm at the surface. Men are silent about who they are as people, sometimes because they have been taught to ignore or suppress their feelings and sometimes because they don't even know they have them. The church has trouble detecting this silence, because this abusive man has learned to be a doer- an achiever- a person who can get things done, especially at work. He has learned that in getting things done, he gets recognition, praise, support even what he thinks is love. Men perform in order to be real men. This is the lesson he has learned from childhood.

I learned at an early age to be busy to succeed. I did well in school, went to church and Sunday School, performed in several choirs, orchestras and bands, and worked as a camp counselor during the summer. I had good parents who taught me successful achievement as the path to recognition. I don't blame them. They were raised in an era when Blacks had to work twice as hard to get half as far.

But in the process, I lost something. To this day, I cannot tell you when I became a human doing instead of a human being. When accomplishment is more important than character, the tendency is to strive for the one at the expense of the other.

I accomplished much fast. I entered college at age 16, graduated valedictorian and entered a Ph.D. program at age twenty. I was teaching at a state college at 22, ordained at 23 and had my choice of plum jobs at 24. I had something else- recognition, attention, and honor…except it wasn't for me.

The accolades were for my performance, not my person; my conquests, not my character. God did not create us to be honored, but loved. I felt a real emptiness because the only way I knew how to get people to pay attention to me was to achieve, and if I achieved and you didn't notice, it hurt and made me angry.

I was a loud visible professional- and a silent invisible person. In retrospect, I didn't know me- the real me- at all. I only knew the precocious professor/preacher who had come so far so fast, and that is who I wanted others to know as well. Many men suffer from the same dilemma. They want approval and acceptance, especially as men who live in a society for what they do rather than what they are. When we are ignored, or not given credit for our actions, it hurts. Unchecked, the hurt turns to anger, the anger to rage and the rage to violence. "Recognize me," is the scream represented in every violent outburst which comes from the man whose work is ignored, whose facade is overlooked, whose image is disrespected.

That image is not the person God loves. God is not interested in the image we create, but the real person inside. Men are notorious for creating fronts, facades designed to project a real image of manliness or machismo when there is a hurting person inside that needs God's love. Satan can work well with this façade. Facades are deceptions, and our enemy is the chief of all deceivers. Men's press to live in this deception- identity based on our professions, not our persons- are prime targets for the wiles of the deceiver. The life lived in such deception and delusion creates a foothold for a stronghold- a place of entry for the enemy to kill, rob and destroy. For this man, violence becomes a way to protect the image of manliness- primarily to ourselves, and also to the abused. "I am a man- no, not a man but the man! I'm in charge- respect me!" So we scream both verbally and physically, like Herod, willing to destroy others in order to affirm our power (see Matthew 2).

Men seek power and authority. In a pure sense, it is part of our created self, God having given authority to humanity in the created order.

That authority was misused when humanity- Adam and Eve- disobeyed the Authority over them, and chose to "be like God," that is, the futile attempt to increase power through its misuse. Violence in the home is an abuse of the power and authority given to humanity. When it seems as if the power of the image we create slips away, violence becomes a way of maintaining the illusion of power, even increasing or intensifying that illusion.

The temptation to misuse power came to Jesus in Luke 4 when He was led into the wilderness by the Spirit. His victory over temptation there brings hope for the violence free living for abusers today. Jesus was first tempted to doubt His identity ("If You are the Son of God…"). God had told Jesus He was the beloved Son, but the doubts now come to Jesus. Similarly, the abuser doubts his manliness, but resistance is available to him. The temptation to make the stones into bread comes to Jesus as an opportunity to use His power to satisfy Himself, but the power given to Him is for the sake of others. The abuser uses his physical power for his own needs- but God has given him that power to bless others. The abuser must not live by bread (physical and psychological need) alone, but by every Word that proceeds from the mouth of God.

The temptation then comes to Jesus to gain power by worshipping Satan. But Satan simply offers a shortcut to the reign that will be

Christ's in the end times, the power without the suffering of the cross. The abuser succumbs to the temptation to gain power without suffering. Jesus' solution to serve God, not Satan and his offer of power, looms as a way of escape for the man who wants to live in peace. The final temptation to Jesus offers the opportunity to use a spectacular demonstration of power to gain a following. The abuser succumbs to the temptation to use physical power to make his mate follow. The church must help the man of rage to declare with Christ that power is not to be tested in such a way. We must have confidence in who God made us to be- who God says we are- rather than try to establish that power through overt activity.

When Jesus submits to God and resists the devil, Satan flees (see also James 5:8). When the abuser is delivered and learns to resist ongoing temptation, he will see Satan flee. But too often, lacking discipline, support and resources, he succumbs when Satan returns at a more opportune time. He goes back to familiar territory of abuse and apology, a deadly cycle both physically and spiritually. Without help, he tries again to reaffirm himself through this violent sense of power. We, the abuser- me, the abuser- struggles when power is threatened the next time. How easy it is to reassert the image in the face of the threat. How easy it is to reclaim bad behaviors when we are not given something new to live by, as opposed to just a one time deliverance experience.

The behaviors continue to mask our helplessness, our fear, and our lack of inherent self worth. God did not send His Son to die for our projections and professions, but our person. The scriptures say that while we were helpless, while we were yet sinners, Christ died for us (Romans 5:6-8). Deliverance meant God peeling back the layers of the image we create-I had created- and learning to walk as the beloved helpless one for whom Christ gave His life.

Deliverance can be instantaneous- a demon cast out, a soul saved or a life miraculously changed. We know that deliverance must be maintained- less the evil return with seven times the intensity. That is why counseling and support are needed for men to maintain a violence free life-style after their conversion or deliverance.

For the delivered abuser to maintain deliverance, their must be support for him as a person. That helpless person for whom Christ died now has the Helper, the Holy Spirit, inside along with the aid of the Scriptures. Without the Spirit working through the community of faith and the Word made flesh in the body of Christ, his journey toward knowing himself is threatened. Who wants to be helpless? Who wants to be weak? Who wants to admit their sinfulness? Who wants to confess their true fears? Now uncovered and delivered, the formerly abusive male looks for space to work through his new life, his ability to live with its insecurities and raw emotions.

Churches that wish to bring reconciliation, deliverance and healing to families plagued by violence must create space for the former perpetrator to heal as well. He needs to be able to talk about his newly discovered helplessness without judgment or condemnation. He needs to know the hope of Christ as it manifests in the testimonies of others who have been delivered from violent behavior. He needs to know that his emotions, now raw with the discovery of his longstanding fears, can be experienced and brought captive to Christ. He needs to know that his worth- now stripped of the violent façade of manliness- is contained in Christ and that we, the body of Christ, recognize that worth. He can be loved uncon-ditionally, even when not performing adequately. He can be supported vigorously, even when he is hurting emotionally. He can be accepted totally, even when his imperfections show. He has put off violence- but what does he put on?

In putting on Christ, the former abuser puts on the qualities of the new life, but he needs help "getting dressed." He joins a family of uncon-ditional love, forgiveness and hope. He joins a family that understands his past sinful history, supports the grace in his present and offers hope for violence free, peace-filled living.

Maintaining deliverance for the formerly abusive male requires real involvement from the body of Christ. I found great strength in people who could identify with my fears and my façade, and yet chose to offer hope, love and friendship rather than condemnation. They let me know that my person, my voice- the real me- had value. They did not excuse my behavior, but offered me forgiveness, their experience of growth in Christ, and their availability to talk if I ever found myself frustrated. Through the power of Christ and His Spirit I have been delivered. Through the resources of the body of Christ, my deliverance is maintained.

Chapter 12

"G.R.A.C.E."

First, we must develop a language that we can all use to understand what domestic violence is, and what is <u>G</u>od's <u>R</u>esponse <u>A</u>t <u>C</u>haotic <u>E</u>vents (G.R.A.C.E.) in the lives of the victim and abuser. Christian ethics and theology purports God's grace, and is the foundation on which we build a bridge to family preservation and reconciliation. This by no means advocates whether a victim and abuser reconciles or divorces. Rather, it lets families know "<u>there's hope</u>" that abusers can correct their abusive behavior and victims can receive the healing, wholeness and render forgiveness at the appointed time. It is important to note that forgiveness and reconciliation can only be made once abusers accept accountability and responsibility for their behavior, and demonstrate their willingness to choose non-violent behaviors.

So we ask, "God, how did we get here?" How did we get to the places in our lives where we feel hopeless and despondent in our family and intimate partner relationships?

We must first start with understanding of our beginning. *In the beginning God created the heavens and the earth. And the earth was waste and empty, and darkness was on the face of the deep, and the Spirit of God was hovering over the face of the waters. (Genesis 1:1-2)* In the book of Genesis, God created the cosmos – a universe that was orderly, harmonious, systematic, complex, and self-inclusive. In other words, God created the universe and included God's self in it. The bible tells us that God created perfect order. God put man in the Garden of Eden and communed with man. From Genesis 1:1-2:25, everything that God made, was good. God had the power and God had the control, but something happened in the garden that turned all humanity and the world to the exact opposite of what God created man and the universe to be.

Nevertheless, God set the stage for man's accountability and responsibility in the beginning. God called Adam to responsibility to account for his whereabouts and for his disobedience, but, Adam blamed Eve. Eve was accused of Adam's downfall. We find this relative norm in domestic violence situations. Perpetrators blaming victims for their abuse.

In Genesis 2:7, *God breathed into the nostrils of man the breath of life, and man became a living soul.* Humanity disobeyed God and God told man if he disobeyed he would surely die, and certainly and unequivocally humanity died (Genesis 3).

God, in the first place (root word primo) or first created (primordial) cosmos with order, but now we have chaos and confusion. God set order and rule in place, but man disobeyed God and the result was chaos. What is chaos? Chaos is a state of things in which chance is supreme. Chaos is the confused, unorganized state of primordial matter before the creation of a distinct form, such as the cosmos. It is a state of utter confusion.

The struggle has since then existed between that which is good and that which is evil. Man's power and control struggling against God's power and control. Hence, today we find humanity trying to exert power and control in their lives and also in the lives of others. What we have are opposites meeting, chaos in a world that God created to be orderly, harmonious, systematic, and included God. Domestic violence and intimate partner violence is a state and cycle of chaos and confusion; utter confusion, disorder, and with every appearance no evidence that God exists.

In exploring the dynamics of domestic violence and interpersonal violence we will come to understand man's quest for power and control. We will understand that domestic violence and interpersonal violence are all about power and control. But we will also come to understand the why's and what is God's response to the chaotic experiences we face, have faced, and ultimately may face in our lives. The issues of our struggles with power and control still face us today, good trying to overcome evil.

What *is* God's response to these chaotic experiences we face in life?

And he said to me, My GRACE suffices thee; for [my] power is perfected in weakness. Most gladly therefore will I rather boast in my weaknesses, that the power of the Christ may dwell upon me. Wherefore I take pleasure in weaknesses, in insults, in necessities, in persecutions, in straits, for Christ: for when I am weak, then I am powerful. 2 Corinthians 12:9-10

Christian faith directs us to God's grace as the answer to our search and quest. Our relationships whether good or evil, have to embrace the concept of G.R.A.C.E. The understanding of what God was saying to me came through a dream. On August 21, 2003, I woke up out of a dream with such pain in my heart. It was about my grandson. He was saying "No, No!" His voice was with such hurt, helplessness, such fear, and such despondency. I just wanted to hurt his abuser like she was hurting him. His little voice kept ringing in my ears! The terror and the frightening cries of this helpless little boy who was being dominated, and having such power and control exerted over him, was disheartening. His little face was filled with terror. I could only say," Oh God, why"? I started to cry because I had such pain, but yet such passion for him, and I knew I had to have that same passion for her. But I couldn't. I did not want to. She had put such hurt and such pain, such fear in this poor little helpless boy. She had damaged him and I would never forgive her. I rolled out of bed to my knees and began to pray, and God responded, *"But if you do not forgive others, your heavenly Father will not forgive you* (Matthew 6:15).

Have you ever imagined the passion and the pain Jesus felt as he was led to Calvary's cross? What is our relationship to Jesus and his response to the pain and the passion that he had toward humankind? What is Jesus' response to passion and pain? Grace is not sitting down and saying, "thank you Lord for the chaos in my life. Bless the hands that are preparing to serve me a black eye, or thank you for this strange touch, and make this violence nourishment for my body. In Jesus name, amen. No, No, No,…Grace is God's unmerited favor towards us, …*in that while we were yet sinners, Christ died* (Roman 5:8).

In the entire New Testament we find GRACE. The Christian believers are living under GRACE and not under the law of the Old Testament. In the New Testament we find the people of God trying to make sense out of how they were to live in a world dominated and controlled by the Roman government and Jesus, their Messiah, had been crucified. There was utter chaos and confusion. Jesus was gone from them physically and they were trying to live out their lives in their own cultures, their own customs, their own laws and the laws of the Roman government as disciples, followers of Jesus Christ.

Today, we are trying to make sense out of our existence, trying to live out our lives in our own cultures, our own customs, and abide by our government's laws. But yet, like people in the Old Testament times we are experiencing some of the same chaotic experiences they faced; Lot & his daughters – incest (Gen. 19:30-38), Amnon & Tamar – rape (2 Sam 13:11-14), Abigail & Nabal – emotional, verbal abuse (1 Sam 25:3), Noah & Ham – drunkenness (Gen 9:21-24), Violence against women – Judges 19:24-25, John 8:3-5, Hosea & Gomer – Hosea, Misuse of scripture – marital rape 1 Cor 7:4, Eph 5:21-33, Cain & Abel – Fratricide (Gen 4:8), and Disobedient son – Deut. 21:18-21, Law of sexual morality – Deut 22:21.

The world is still in chaos. As in bible days, we as Christian believers have experienced African slavery, the Holocaust, World Wars I & II, fratricide, patricide, terrorism and other events that humanity is inflicting upon one another because of power and control issues.

Nonetheless, in the book of Ephesians 4:22-32, God gives us direction in our relationships toward one another.

> ...if ye have heard him and been instructed in him according as [the] truth is in Jesus; [namely] your having put off according to the former conversation the old man which corrupts itself according to the deceitful lusts: and being renewed in the spirit of your mind; and [your] having put on the new man, which according to God is created in truthful

*righteousness and holiness. Wherefore, having put off falsehood, speak truth every one with his neighbor, because we are members one of another. Be angry, and do not sin; let not the sun set upon your wrath, neither give room for the devil. Let the stealer steal no more, but rather let him toil, working what is honest with [his] hands, that he may have to distribute to him that has need. Let no corrupt word go out of your mouth, but if [there be] any good one for needful. And do not grieve the Holy Spirit of God, with which ye have been sealed for [the] day of redemption. Let all bitterness, and heat of passion, and wrath, and clamour, and injurious language, be removed from you, with all malice; and be to one another kind, compassionate, forgiving one another, so as God also in Christ has forgiven you. **Ephesians 4:22-32** Young's Literal Translation*

According to Ephesians, human existence is beset by the malevolent (showing vicious and intense ill will, spite and hatred) influence of demonic beings. Christ has been given power over them, and through God's GRACE humanity may be freed from their immoral (violent) and deceitful influences. Paul is appealing to the church and to us to maintain unity in our families and in relationship with one another by rejecting the former lifestyles of violence, hatred, bigotry, and dissensions. Because of our desire to exert power and control, rather than advocating a complete renewal of family relationships based on love, forgiveness, and mutual submission. Paul uses his own Christology or understanding of Christ to justify the structure and duties of the ancient patriarchal family. We have to remember the culture and times of biblical writing. We have to be re-socialized into God's purpose for the family. Once alienated, lost, strangers to covenant (Colossians 2:12-13), we are now being shown the depiction of a relationship within the household of God.

...submitting yourselves to one another in [the] fear of Christ. Wives, [submit yourselves] to your own husbands, as to the Lord, for a husband is head of the wife, as also the Christ [is] head of the assembly. *He* [is] Saviour of the body. But even as the assembly is subjected to the Christ, so also wives to their own husbands in everything. Husbands, love your own wives, even as the Christ also loved the assembly, and has delivered himself up for it, in order that he might sanctify it, purifying [it] by the washing of water by [the] word, that *he* might present the assembly to himself glorious, having no spot, or wrinkle, or any of such things; but that it might be holy and blameless. So ought men also to love their own wives as their own bodies: he that loves his own wife loves himself. For no one has ever hated his own flesh, but nourishes and cherishes it, even as also the Christ the assembly: for we are members of his body; [we are of his flesh, and of his bones.] Because of this a man shall leave his father and mother, and shall be united to his wife, and the two shall be one flesh. This mystery is great, but *I* speak as to Christ, and as to the assembly. But *ye* also, every one of you, let each so love his own wife as himself; but as to the wife [I speak] that she may fear the husband. **Ephesians 5:21-31 Darby's Translation**

In Ephesians 5:21-32, including Ephesians 6:1-2, God gives perspective to children, and the relationship between married persons should mirror the one between Christ and the church. Mutuality of husband and wife is affirmed. It is noted by theologians that in the undisputed Pauline letters there is no mention of a wife's subjection or subordination. No matter how wretched we once were, we (all humanity) have equal privileges.

For so many years this scripture has been used to subjugate women and children. In other words dominate, exert power and control over them. The bible tells us in Ephesians 4:14-17, that we are no longer to be tossed to and fro and carried about with every wind of doctrine and belief and interpretation about woman's subjection to man, but understand the truth for ourselves and the relationship that God desires for us to have with one another. It's about GRACE.

And so, even in the midst of our chaos, with our own interpretations, and our own truths, GOD will speak.

We may not have come into the understanding and context of how God intended us to use the example of Eph 5:21-32, but, in its correct context, it is put forth as a man's and a woman's mutual love, reverence and respect they should have toward one another as Christ loves, cherishes, reverences, and respects the church. Our relationships to one another are signified by an analogy that was written as the relationship between Christ and the Church. Domestic violence in the family is not what God intended for the family; however, his response is still G.R.A.C.E. It's all about GRACE.

God's **R**ichest **A**t **C**hrist's **E**xpense. Oh, what love God had for me that he gave his life. God's response to the chaotic experiences in our lives is looking beyond our faults and seeing our need. Our need for forgiveness, our need for grace, and our need for mercy. Some would argue that mercy in domestic violence situations would not be applicable because there is no expectation of the abuser to change, but to throw him or her on the mercy of the court, if you will. However, we could argue this same case with grace. God's grace is unmerited favor and given to all, although we are undeserving; as well as not always motivated to change dysfunctional and sinful behavior. Whether the abuser or the abused, everyone needs some grace and they need some M.E.R.C.Y (**M**e **E**xpecting **R**econciliation **C**ontinuously, **Y**et)…You notice the three dots after yet, well what does it mean? In our relationship with God we all expect reconciliation continuously yet, we are unfaithful, yet, we are disobedient, yet, I am beating my wife, yet, I am sexually abusing my children, yet, I am….This is no admonishment that a victim has to suck it all up and be tough. As the faith community we ultimately want every victim of domestic violence and intimate partner violence to be safe. The day has to come that forgiveness and reconciliation be granted grace and mercy, just as we want God to give us grace and mercy. This is a hard saying and many may not be able to receive this message.

The sinfulness of sin brings us to the realization of God's mercy and grace and the acceptance and forgiveness we must have for others. When we recognize our own sinfulness, we cannot help but plead for restorative love, mercy, kindness, compassion, and grace for ourselves. Much more, Christians should stand in the gap for others who have fallen from fellowship with God and also long for reconciliation and restoration. Robert Foster says, "He who has been forgiven much, will give so much more." We have these examples demonstrated in Mary Magdalene who had seven demons cast out by Jesus. Look at the witness and testimony that is still being told of her faithfulness and ministry to Jesus during His life and after His death (Matthew). Paul, a persecutor of the church, was an accuser of the brethren of the church of Christ. Paul became the writer of a major portion of the writings of the New Testament books of the bible . Peter, who denied Christ, became an apostle and leader in the church. Peter's renowned sermons added great numbers of believers to the church daily (Acts). As believers in Christ, we stand in Christ's stead forgiving or retaining the sins of others. Matthew 18:13-22 gives us a perspective of releasing those who have fallen into disagreement and the proper response of forgiveness and restoration.

We must come to the knowledge and understanding that God's response to our questions are found by establishing a relationship with Him first. When we come to understand that God is in control of all things and we can submit to him; then we can find room to establish a relationship with others that will be healthy and wholesome.

When we have healthy and wholesome relationships with one another in our families, or other intimate relationships, we will no longer take part in the sins of others. There are many ways we abet or take part in domestic violence and intimate partner violence as the abused. There are many ways of abetting or taking part in the sins of others. First, through commendation, victims believe they are worthy of being beaten and they deserved it. Next, through counsel, the victim gives thought to and believe within themselves the violence is justified. Third, through consent, the victim says, " it's ok to beat me, hurt me," allowing the abuse to continue. Last, through concealment, in which the victim remains silent, he/she hides the abuse.

And if we, the faith community, specifically the church, share with others their sins, we must expect to share in their plagues. If we do not reprove the violence and stop the violence, or break the silence, then we have consented to this breach in God's purpose for our lives. The faith community must begin to break the traditional and cultural boundaries of women and children domination, marginalization, and discrimination. These boundaries Jesus broke through were mere exercises of G.R.A.C.E

Jesus is the revelation of who God is and what God's response would be to every situation we can encounter in life; even domestic violence and abuse. We don't have to fight for power and control over one another. God has given us power and authority over everything that God has made. He who the son sets free is free indeed (John 8:36). Victims nor abusers have to be bound by the cycle of abuse and violence. As collaborative efforts of church and state, we must break the silence of abuse and strengthen family ties through open communication, caring, confrontation, and counsel.

We have a love and duty to one another that is signified by Christ's love for the church. Ephesians 5:21-32 clearly gives us the mandate and the law for relationships. Relationships that are not of dominance and power, but of mutual subjection, love, reverence, and respect.

In conclusion, our response to perpetrators of domestic violence is to give hope of transforming initiatives that will replace old behaviors, old practices, and old ideologies of imprisonment, but conversely, training, counseling, and therapy to reverse learned behavior of violence and replace with behavior of peacemaking and truth telling. Our responsibilities as part of the faith community is to find ways and means to help men and women find gainful employment to take care of their families, educate and train them on problem solving skills, and teach them how to have healthy relationships. We must teach about gender, a concept that refers to the social differences, as opposed to the biological ones, between women and men that have been learned, are changeable over time, and have wide variations both within and between cultures. Gender analyses must be conducted to help understand the impact of disparities people face in society.

Evaluations and audits must be held in order to understand how policies, programs and institutional practices affect the ability of persons to exist in their own societies and cultures. Failing to address the gender dimensions of our society breeds gender based violence and perpetuation of the cycle of violence.

We will replace dysfunctional theology and ethics with an ethical Christology of responsibility and accountability to each other. Jesus, whose ministry and purpose was to bring liberation and salvation to all, has given us the same ministry of reconciliation by taking the liberating news of the gospel to the whole world. As ambassadors for Christ, we must not hold to the view that one is to dominate, brutalize, terrorize, nor control another human being. Rather we are to be in harmony with God and with one another. The action and call of God is transcendent and goes beyond any institutionalized organization.

When we fail to bring healing and wholeness to all of God's creatures, the image of God is tarnished. We are charged to recognize that which is sick and broken, call it by name, and attempt to fix it. When we have done so, we are on the way to conscientiously being in the likeness and taking on the image of God, recognizing the need for healing. Jesus demonstrated what being in the image of God meant.

There is hope that perpetrators of violence towards men, women and children can one day walk in the newness of life, forgetting those things that are behind, and reaching for those things that are in the future. The promise of God, *"if any man be in Christ, he is a new creature, old things are passed away and behold all things are become new"* **2 Corinthians 5:17**.

Chapter 13

"BEYOND THE CRISIS- HOPE FOR TOMORROW"

*Now faith is the substance of things **hoped** for, the evidence of things not seen.*

Hebrews 11:1

Using the word hope in a casual conversation, it may sound as if you are wavering and uncertain about that which you want to obtain or do. The hope of which I speak focuses on God and is filled with earnest expectation. No one whose hope is in God will ever be overcome by disappointment, but will be filled with patience, encouragement, and enthusiasm. You notice I did not say that you will not be disappointed, but that you will not be overcome (conquered, defeated, triumphed over) with disappointment. As a matter of fact, in this life you will suffer hardships, trials, tribulations, and persecutions. Nevertheless, the hope we have is as an anchor of the soul, both sure and steadfast (Hebrews 6:19a). This hope gives us courage to face each new day.

There were many days I didn't think I would make it through the day nor want to face what tomorrow would bring. Court dates, doctor visits, hospital visits, filing police reports, caring for my children, worrying if

bills would be paid, trying to help somebody else when I wanted someone to help me, and trying to keep a sane mind all at the same time, one
could easily give up and give in to defeat. Because I knew God and trusted God, I could say as the psalmist says,

> *And I continually do wait with hope, And have added unto all Thy*
> *praise.* **Psalm 71:14**

Even though there were days I was afraid of what tomorrow would
bring, I had to muster the courage to keep going. It seemed like there was
always something to do or something that happened to keep pulling me
down. My life was wrapped up in trying to spare my children any more
hurt and suffering. Yet, I didn't realize I couldn't do it alone. Only with
God as my helper and Jesus Christ as my savior was I able to push ahead.
For it is both God and His Son, Jesus Christ that Christian hope depends.
The promises of God, the God who is the same yesterday, today, and forever, is the same God who holds our tomorrows.

What is tomorrow? Tomorrow is defined as the day after today. So if
we want to understand our hope for tomorrow, we must understand our
today. Today is the present. I had my now moment and my due time, and
now I had to face my today and respond in obedience or disobedience.
You see, todays have theological implications of God's timing. Our today
is marked by moments of opportunities to hear God's voice speak words

of guidance and directions for the day.

Today is an opportunity to plant a seed. If I capitalize on the moment, if I take the initiative to educate, equip, and empower someone today, then the day after today, that person may be alive. That person may be able to tell someone else about their abuse. That person is able to have another day to gain the courage to say, "no more." A seed planted in the ground today is a meal for a family tomorrow. A seed planted today is a harvest for tomorrow.

Like the farmers who plant their crops today, they hope tomorrow will bring them an increase. That's how we have to be as we work with both victims and perpetrators of domestic violence and abuse. The grains of information we share, the helping hands we extend, the listening ear we offer, and the justice and mercy we seek today, gives hope to victims and the opportunity to be able to walk free from abuse, or for perpetrators to get the help they need to stop battering or inflicting violence. The yield may be thirty fold, sixty fold, or a hundred fold increase in the survival rates. What does that mean? It means the opportunities we make use of may save thirty victims from dying, or sixty perpetrators from battering again, or a hundred families reconciled and not torn apart. Ultimately, we want to reduce the rate of recidivism; hoping that those we help today will not return to their abuse tomorrow.

Therefore our message of "hope for tomorrow" must be strong, persuasive, and encouraging. Our message must relay the hope that healing, wholeness, reconciliation, and preservation of the family is possible. Nonetheless, my hope and your hope for tomorrow, whether for the good, or the absence of the bad, we hope.

Reverend Jessie Jackson in the 60's or 70's coined the phrase, "keep hope alive". Hope just may keep a victim alive long enough to walk away safe in his or her freedom. Hope, like grace, is what woke you and me up this morning not knowing what the day would bring. Hope keeps us moving towards our goals and to never give up until victory has been reached. Hope helps us deal with persevering to see the potential in our children come to fruition; never giving up hope that the violence and abuse will not immobilize them forever. Hope is the driving force behind every victim who believes their perpetrator or abuser may change and stop the violence.

We have the assurance that we are not defeated nor are we overcome by the enemy. Know the truth of the Word of God for yourself. Seek godly counsel, but know that God has not given you a mandate to suffer violence and abuse at the hands of another human being. God has not given us the mandate to be treated like a doormat or less than human.

Today, we can no longer abet or take part in the sin of abuse. There are many ways we along with others take part in our own abuse. First, through commendation, as we believe we are worthy of being beaten and deserve it. Next, through counsel, we give thought to and believe within ourselves the violence and abuse is justified. Third, we consent, as we say, "it's okay to beat me, to hurt me" by allowing the abuse to continue. Last, through concealment, as we remain silent and hide the abuse.

Everyone, everywhere, specifically the faith-communities, must reprove and stop the violence, break the silence and not allow this breach in God's purpose for our lives.

When we hear God's voice, the writer of Hebrews tells us, "Today if ye will hear his voice, harden not your hearts." In other words, when God speaks, we are to respond with faith's obedience and thus step into a personal experience of God's rest. Today is that personal confrontation that one has with God as God unveils His will. It is only through our obedience today that will give us hope for tomorrow; the hope and assurance to know that God's rest awaits us.

Domestic violence and abuse are tiring. I have never felt so tired and so drained in all my life. The weight of thirteen spirits being attached to you everyday for twenty-three years, would make a strong man tired. But God's mercy did not let me be consumed. My response and your response to God's today encounter will determine your earnest expectation (hope) of tomorrow. If we listen and obey God's voice, we will find rest and peace. This is the promise that God has given to us. If tomorrow is the day after today, then the day after we respond to God's encounter, we have rest.

You and I will know hurt and uncertain tomorrows. We may suffer and experience the tragedy of domestic violence and abuse, yet we can face our tomorrows expectantly. We may have to wait a while for the full experience of the good that God intends for us, but God is fully committed to everyone who makes a faith commitment to Him. As long as our hope is in God and His Son, Jesus Christ, we have hope and a tomorrow; a tomorrow of victory and the anticipation that tomorrow will be a better day than today.

Notes

1 Expository Dictionary of Bible Words, p.598

EPILOGUE

What should Christians believe about the work of Christ and God's forgiveness?

Jesus Christ is the central point of belief that all aspects of Christian faith are illumined.[1] As Christian believers, one should believe as professed in the Apostle's Creed, the affirmation that Jesus is the Son of God and the Savior of the world. Jesus, fully human and fully divine, was born a Jew, experienced human need and human limitations, was tempted to sin, but was without sin, and was the sacrificial offering God gave that humankind would be forgiven of their transgressions against God. Christians should believe that humankind has been separated from God because of sin (Romans 3:23) and that it was to the call for forgiveness and reconciliation that Jesus came (II Corinthians 5:19).

This is the saving work of Jesus Christ. It is about God acting first, taking the initiative to make peace with humanity because of God's love for us. Not that we deserved, nor could earn God's forgiveness, but, God forgave us in spite of ourselves. Not that we loved God but God first loved us.

The theme of forgiveness was marked by Jesus' ministry and was a decisive characteristic of his own teaching, activity, and self-identification.[2] The forgiveness of sin was a critical feature of the kingdom of God to which Jesus attested. In fact, Jesus' own death on the cross was in view of the sinfulness, violence, and destruction that were part and parcel of our social, economic, political and domestic life. The finished work at the cross sealed God's forgiveness to humankind and paid the penalty of death that sin required (Romans 6:23). Even on the cross, Jesus asked God to forgive those who crucified Him (Luke 23:34).

Jesus' shed blood was the atonement for our sin. "*At one moment*" Jesus' sacrificial death emphasized the seriousness of our sin and the extent to which God poured out God's love on us (Romans 5:8). Jesus' work disrupts the order of a sinful world by announcing the forgiveness of sinners and calling whosoever would hear and believe to repent and receive a new way of life characterized by the love of God.

It is only God that has the power to forgive sin. Yet, Jesus Christ, God incarnate, wrapped in human flesh, became the free gift of God so that humankind would be forgiven. Without Jesus Christ and the works that He completed, there would be no forgiveness of sin nor reconciliation between God and humankind (Hebrews 9:22).

God's forgiveness is still applicable for the Christian believer today. Who we believe Jesus to be for us today must be examined by every believer. The Christian believer has the assurance that Jesus' work at the cross still covers the sins of the world. Because of this, Christian believers should believe that the same ministry of reconciliation and forgiveness that Jesus preached and taught is the same ministry of reconciliation to which Christian believers are called. Our responsibility is to be ambassadors for Christ, spreading the gospel of Jesus Christ and God's love for all humankind. *For God so loved the world, that He gave His only begotten Son; that whosoever believeth in Him should not perish, but have everlasting life (John 3:16).*

How to explain forgiveness and the relationship between God the Holy Spirit and the human spirit?

The Bible tells us that we, humanity, were made in the image of God (Imago De). This belief of being in the likeness of God is understood as an unfolding of character to which we are evolving, constantly moving toward, and will only come to its full manifestation in the end times. Although we are made of flesh and blood, being in the image of God reminds us that we are also spiritual beings. The dynamics of our spiritual selves give us the ability to think, understand, use our imagination, memory, reason, and receive revelations of who God is and our relationship with God.

Our ability to have relationship with God is made possible by God the Holy Spirit, the third person of the Holy Trinity. The relationship between God, the Holy Spirit, and the human spirit is the Holy Spirit is the divine, transforming agent that transforms the human spirit and makes it possible to have a relationship and fellowship with God. The Holy Spirit ensures us that the love of God is still working to transform humanity to that which God created them to be.

We see the manifestation of God the Holy Spirit at work in the human spirit of the believer as the Holy Spirit empowers the believer to live out the commandments of God and to do the work of the ministry to which they have been called out in Jesus Christ, and to a broken world. This empowerment by the Spirit enables the Christian believer to live in unity with Christ, each other, and in community fellowship with other believers. The Gifts of the Spirit are given to the believer to help heal the wounded human spirits of humanity that are constantly at war within us and the forces working outside us. The Holy Spirit is at work in us, converting the frailties of the human spirit to a new life in Christ. It replaces bitterness, wrath, malice, hatred, indifference, bigotry, and other works of the flesh with the love of God and the Fruit of the Spirit. As we become conscious of the brokenness of the world and try to fix that which is broken, we move towards the reality of being in the image of God. The Holy Spirit brings that transformation.

Christians believe that sin in the world brought judgment and death; and upon confession of faith in Jesus Christ, the Holy Spirit would bring regeneration and renewal of life. This renewal causes us to look outside ourselves, not to be self-centered; but rather, to look outside ourselves to a world in need. We recognize that in the world things are not as they ought to be, the world has no power of itself to help itself nor to free itself, and the help that is needed in the world has to come from those God has empowered with the Holy Spirit to bring about the change. Thus, self-centeredness becomes Christ-centered and God-centeredness. This act of self-denial liberates us from the personal and political system-atic structures that keep people in bondage.

Jesus promised that He would send the comforter, which is the Holy Spirit to be the active presence of God in the believers' life, community, and the world (John 15:26 – 16:7).

When and how does forgiveness apply to domestic violence and abuse?

Victims of domestic violence and abuse may have experienced trau-matic situations. This trauma can be psychologically and emotionally damaging to a victim. While Jesus calls us to forgive those that trespass against us, we realize that the path to forgiving someone who has been abusive and violent, may take time. Each individual is different and each case requires individual consideration. Often times, rushing to forgive the trespass prohibits or gets in the way of the accountability and responsibility we each have towards God and our fellow human being. Seek God, professional Christian counseling, and pastoral counseling as you move towards your complete healing. Never let anyone push you into quick forgiveness if you are not ready. It is better to be truthful about where you are on the scope of forgiveness rather than lie and cause yourself to be re-victimized again because of trying to please someone else. Remember it was you who went through, not them. They do not know how you felt, what you went through, or what you are going through now as you seek your healing. Trust the God within you. God says, "I will never leave you nor forsake you."

Why is belief in the Resurrection crucial to our Christian existence?

The resurrection of Jesus Christ has been the most important aspect of Jesus' life for the Christian believer. It is part of the Christian's profession of faith as written in the Apostle's Creed that God raised the crucified Jesus from the dead. Without the resurrection, the gospel message would have been incomplete, and Jesus would have been another religious prophet who did great works, lived a good life and died. However, it is the resurrection of Jesus that sets Him apart unlike any of the other prophets that came to deliver God's message of love, peace and reconciliation. It indeed signifies the divinity of Jesus and confirms that Jesus was who he claimed to be, the Son of God.

It is only the Son of God that can vindicate humanity from the penalty of sin and death. The history of the Christian church shows believers have been worshipping the resurrected Christ for centuries. The soteriological implications of the resurrection affirm our being saved from eternal death and living in right relationship with God. The eschatological implications assure us that physical death will not separate us from the constancy of God's love. By *God's mercy we have an inheritance that is incorruptible, and undefiled, and that fadeth not away, and is reserved in heaven for us (1Peter 1:3-4)*. For the Christian believer, the resurrection represents life after death of the physical body and the promise of living with God eternally. It establishes and under-girds the Christian hope. For those who have died believing in Jesus Christ, the Christian hope is that one day all believers will be reunited.

Although there is no scientific evidence of the resurrection, eyewitness accounts by Jesus' disciples and the apostles have promulgated through thousands of years of history and have been accepted as truth by faith. An empty tomb where Jesus was to have been buried, further gave credence to the historical evidence that Jesus died, but no one could produce His body. Jesus is the first-fruit of them that sleep, and of whom God raised from the dead and the promise is to us that one day we shall be like Jesus.

Without the resurrection of Christ, our faith would be in vain (1 Corinthians 15:11-29). We would be a people without hope, and destined to a life of pain, suffering, and left to die in our sins. The good news of the gospel of Christ has to include the victory that Christ gained over sin and death in this life and the life to come. It is the affirmation of the victory God gained in Jesus Christ for all humanity to be reconciled back to God. Victory over death and the grave is tantamount to the Christian believer's faith that rests in the assurance that Jesus Christ defeated the power of sin and its consequences over our lives. That same resurrection power that Christ gained is given to us to go into the world to teach and preach the gospel of Jesus Christ (Matthew 28:18-20).

AFTERWORD

In order for domestic violence to be stopped, it must be exposed. Rev. Maxine Lloyd Ball has done so, with power, sensitivity, transparency and hope. Her words here tell an important and, unfortunately, not uncommon story. But it is a story that must be told, in order for others to find hope for deliverance.

In 1983, Marie Marshall Fortune penned <u>Sexual Violence: The Unmentionable Sin</u>. This groundbreaking work began an important conversation in the Christian church about domestic violence. Fortune called it "the unmentionable sin" because the church had been silent about its existence. In order for Christians to address this horrific sin and its consequence it had to be exposed. In order for the church to minister to victims and bring justice and healing to all concerned, the sin must be mentioned. In subsequent years, more has been written, more testimonies given and more healing and justice available.

Maxine Lloyd Ball's story is a critical part of the process of making the unmentionable mentionable. Moreover, her ability to bring together the spiritual need for deliverance, the psychological need for counseling and the social need for interpersonal support reflect a holistic understanding of the Gospel of Jesus Christ, by whose death and resurrection we find healing in all three areas. Too often, the church has treated this solely as a spiritual condition with deliverance as the goal, but no psychological or social support. Others treat the psychological issues without attending to the spirit realm. Others provide social support, but without dealing with the demonic influence and psychological damage. Rev Lloyd Ball recognizes that we are spirit, soul and body, and presents a model for diagnosis, deliverance and development that addresses the total person. In allowing me to contribute a chapter that deals honestly and hopefully about the redemption of abusers, she has demonstrated her commitment to full reconciliation as the highest good in the Kingdom, but without compromising the safety of victims, nor excusing the behavior of perpetrators.

If you are a pastor or church leader, know that there are women in your congregation who have suffered from violence and abuse. They are silent- they do not feel that they have permission to tell their story. They are intimidated by shame, our history of blaming victims, and fear of isolation and ostracism. Jesus would not shrink back from such victims and neither should we.

Know also that as a church leader, you should avail yourself of as many support systems as necessary to help victims of domestic violence. Know where the battered women's shelters are. Know the safe places women can be referred. Know the professionals who can provide counsel consistent with your church's doctrine. Know resources such as the FaithTrust Institute (www.faithtrust.org) and Isaac Ministries (www.mlministries.org) that provide further education and training for clergy and church leaders. Know where perpetrators can receive help. Know the criminal justice system and its available resources. Know your local domestic violence prevention organizations. And above all, know that Jesus holds us accountable for how we treat victims.

Rev. Maxine Lloyd Ball's writing on this issue should press us all to be more vigilant in addressing this evil in church and society. We are in her debt.

Harold Dean Trulear, Ph.D.,
Associate Professor of Applied Theology,
Howard University School of Divinity

APPENDIX A

SAFETY PLAN

Guide taken from The Family Crisis Center of Prince George's County, Shelter for Battered Women

SAFETY MEASURES WHILE YOU'RE IN AN ABUSIVE RELATIONSHIP

Whether you stay or go you will be safer if you have an escape plan. A safety plan is a plan of action designed to help keep victims and their families as safe as possible.

Memorize the Family Crisis Center Domestic Violence Hotline number or the hotline number for shelters for battered women and children in your area——(301) 731-1203. The hotline is the initial point of contact for the services. It renders immediate access to safe housing for women and their children fleeing violence in their homes, information for court-mandated victims, the safe visitation center, the legal advocacy program and dissemination of information about additional services in the Maryland, Washington DC and Virginia areas. Each area's services provided may differ.

Keep other important phone numbers handy —such as police, friends, or taxi companies.

Tell as many of your friends and neighbors as you safely can — Don't cooperate in your abuse by keeping it a secret. Have people listening for unusual disturbances and ready to call the police.

Establish a code word or sign so that family, friends and co-workers know when to call for help.

Discuss safety planning with your children, if they are old enough. Teach them important phone numbers, including when and how to dial 911.

If you can open your own bank account. Save as much money as possible.

Try not to let your abuser trap you in the kitchen (too many potential weapons) **or the bathroom** (no space to dodge blows and too many hard surfaces to be pushed or knocked against). Think about the safest rooms in your house or apartment and try to stay there during an argument. Leave if you can safely do so.

Stay our of a room or area where there are known weapons such as guns. Do not attempt to threaten him/her with a weapon —- it can easily be turned against you.

Think through now, before the attack, just where you will go. The best choice is to the home of someone who cares for you and will support you no matter what you do. If you have no safe friends or family, consider a shelter. At the very least, to a public place. Know where the closest police or fire station is.

Before the next incident, get an extra car key made and hide it in or on the car. You can purchase an inexpensive magnet key holder at a drug store or hardware store.

Keep some extra money for transportation/phone outside of the home in an accessible location.

If you can't afford a cell phone, talk with programs and organizations that may allow you to borrow a cell phone to be able to call 911.

Pack an extra set of clothes and shoes for yourself and your children: include diapers, toiletries, and a bit of money. Store these with a neighbor, friend or a church if you are not planning to leave immediately.

Gather and photocopy important documents you might need: such as birth certificates, social security numbers, utility receipts, checking and saving account books, credit cards, account numbers, passports, marriage license, medical insurance information, important phone numbers, children's school records, deed or lease agreement for the apartment or house, and evidence of abuse and other information you may feel is necessary. Keep these copies outside of your home.

Safety after you have left the relationship

Change your phone number and screen your calls

Change your locks.

Install as many security features as possible in your home.

Inform neighbors that your former partner is not welcome on the premises. Ask them to call the police if they see any person loitering about your property or watching your home.

Make sure the people who care for your children are very clear about who does and who does not have permission to pick up your children.

Let your co-workers know about the situation, and ask them to warn you if they observe that person around

Avoid the stores, banks, and businesses you used when you were living with the abuser

Vary your routine in case the abuser decides to follow you.

Get Counseling. Attend workshops. Join support groups. Do whatever it takes to form a supportive network that will be there when you need it.

APPENDIX B

BOOK LIST

A Soldier Looks at Spiritual Warfare, by Dick Denny

Armed and Dangerous, by Ken Abraham

By Jesus' 39 Stripes We Were Healed, by Walt Straughan

Do it Afraid, by Joyce Meyer

Don't Die in the Winter, by Dr. Millicent Hunter

Faith Seeking Understanding, by Daniel L. Migliore

God's Answers for Your Life

God's Creative Power Will Work for You

MasterLife: The Disciples Victory, by Avery T. Willis, Jr.

Pedagogy of the Oppressed, by Paul Freire

Piercing the Darkness, by Frank Perritti

Pigs in the Parlor, by Frank and Ida Mae Hammond

Strongman's His Name…What's His Game, by Drs. Jerry & Carol Robeson

The Be Happy Attitudes, by Robert Schuller

The Names of God, by Lester Sumrall

This is Your Day for a Miracle, by Benny Hinn

This Present Darkness, by Frank Perritti

GLOSSARY OF TERMS

Abuse: Can be any of the following:
an act that causes serious bodily harm; an act that places a person eligible for relief in fear of imminent serious bodily harm; assault in any degree; rape or sexual offense; false imprisonment; or child abuse or vulnerable adult abuse.

Advocacy: Is a political process consisting of actions designed to transform citizen or popular interests into rights; a process aimed at influencing decisions regarding policies and laws at national and international levels; actions designed to draw a community's attention to an issue and to direct policy makers to a solution.

Advocacy and Case Management (Advocacy): This term indicates that there will be a person assisting you with your individual case. This person may or may not be an attorney or a licensed therapist; this person may be a volunteer.

Assessment: Broadly, an evaluative process of identifying and defining needs. Numerous types of assessment exist including, but not limited to, technical assistance, psychosocial, medical, community and risk assessments.

Batterer's Program (Abuse Intervention Program): This term does NOT indicate that the person who hurt you will be in the same program or will receive treatment in the same Center or Facility. This type of program is designed to promote victim safety by holding batterers accountable for their behavior in order to eliminate violent and coercive acts against an intimate partner. These programs try to educate batterers and give them skills to help cope and manage their anger.

Case-Analysis: Process of assessing system response to children and families by collecting information on case flow through and across different agencies such as police departments, child protective services, prosecutor's office, courts, human service agencies, and intervention and treatment providers. Case analysis is an analytical tool that is individualized to each community. Existing data sources are used to assess such aspects of system operation as timelines of response, referrals to service providers, case "recidivism" (that is, re-entry of child or family into system after case closure), and case dispositions. Through sample analysis at varying points of time, communities can also examine trends such as increases or decreases in types of cases and their dispositions.

Cohabitant: A person who has had sexual relations with the respondent at any time and lived with the respondent for at least ninety (90) days within the past year. The ninety (90) days do not have to be consecutive. Spending the night with the respondent at least ninety (90) times in the past year also qualifies you as a cohabitant (that is, 90 days in a row).

Collaboration: A mutually beneficial well-defined relationship entered into by two or more organizations to achieve common goals. Collaboration is the process of various individuals, groups, or systems working together but at a significantly higher degree than through coordination or cooperation. Collaboration typically involves joint planning, shared resources, and joint resource management. Collaboration occurs through shared understanding of the issues, open communication, mutual trust, and tolerance of differing points of view. To collaborate is to "co-labor."

Community Assessment: An evaluative study that uses objective data to assess the current social conditions of a specified community or targeted area.

Community Education/Outreach/Professional Education: Programs out in the community that attempt to change societal attitudes about domestic violence through presentations and/or speakers. Centers often reach out to the communities where they are located in order to promote understanding and knowledge about domestic violence and sexual assault.

Court Accompaniment: This term indicates that a person will accompany you to court for proceedings that relate to your case (i.e. protective order hearing). This person may or may not be a lawyer.

Direct Representation: This term indicates that you will have an attorney working for you on your individual case.

Domestic Violence: Domestic violence is abusive behavior used by one person in an intimate relationship to maintain power and control over another. It is exerted through physical, psychological, and or economic means.

Emergency Family Maintenance: A monetary award that the Judge can order when the respondent has a duty to support his/her spouse or child (ren). The award will last for the duration of the Protective Order. When the Protective Order ends, the emergency Family Maintenance will end as well.

Exposure to Violence: Exposure includes witnessing (through domestic violence or community violence) or experiencing (through child abuse and neglect) a violent incident(s) by a child in their home or community.

Family Law: This term refers to the legal issues other than ex parte or protective order hearings. Family law cases consist of divorce, legal separation, child custody, and child support, and related issues.

Final Protective Order (FPO):   Official decision issued by the Court after a hearing regarding the alleged abuse. Protective Orders may be awarded with the consent of the respondent *or* after a hearing. Protective Orders can be issued for up to one year. The Final Protective Order can require a respondent not to abuse, threaten or contact the petitioner.   These orders can also cover custody, visitation, emergency family maintenance, use and possession of a home and/or vehicle, counseling, and surrender of firearms.

First Responders: Emergency personnel called to the scene of a crisis or responding to emergency calls for assistance. First responders could include emergency medical technicians, police, hotline/crisis line personnel; fire and rescue; child protective services and others.

Gender: A concept that refers to the social differences, as opposed to the biological ones, between women and men that have been learned, are changeable over time, and have wide variations both within and between cultures.

Gender Analysis: The study of differences in the conditions, needs, participation rates, access to resources and development, control of assets, decision-making powers, etc., between women and men in their assigned gender roles.

Gender Audit: The analysis and evaluation of policies, programs and institutions in terms of how they apply gender-related criteria.

Gender Based Violence/Sexual Violence: Any form of violence by use or threat of physical or emotional force, including rape, wife battering, sexual harassment, incest and pedophilia.

Gender Blind: Ignoring/failing to address the gender dimension (as opposed to gender sensitive or gender neutral).

Impact of Children Exposed to Violence: The impact of children exposed to violence, any consequence short or long-term, both positive and negative, of the child or family being exposed to violence, either as victims or witnesses. Typically, however, impacts of exposure to violence are implicitly taken as a negative effect. The impact can be evident at multiple levels including the individual, the family, and the community. Systemic and cultural issues are important contextual aspects. The impact on children can be observed as threats to their biological, cognitive, emotional, educational, social, and psychological development.

Individual/Family Assessment: A practice skill and process used in working with individuals or families when a "case" is developed to identify the current social, emotional, psychological, and physical conditions of the individual or family. This assessment process can be conducted both formally or informally depending on the nature and setting of service. Clinical settings require formal assessments using specific, validated tools or instruments. From a research perspective, a client-level assessment is an evaluative study that uses objective data to assess the current social, emotional, psychological, and physical conditions of an individual or family.

Interim Protective Order (IPO): A special order that provides emergency domestic violence protection during hours when the courts are closed. The order lasts up to 48 hours until the courts reopen. You must appear in district court for a Temporary Protective Order to extend the protection. The order can be issued by the District Court Commissioner at night and during weekends.

Intervention: Specific services, activities or products developed and implemented to change or improve program participants' knowledge, attitudes, behavior or awareness. Intervention is a purposeful response to an event where a child was exposed to violence. The intervention can be acute, when services are provided at the scene of the exposure, or the intervention can be provided after the event has already occurred. Interventions can take many forms and involve the action of a variety of professionals. Clinicians, teachers, parents, clergy, police, courts, and a variety of other individuals may provide interventions. The goals of an intervention are at least two: to provide support to the individual or persons who have been affected by the exposure to violence, and to find immediate solutions to practical problems that arise from, or gave rise to, the traumatic, disruptive, violent experience.

Lawyer Referrals: This term indicates that service providers will help victims locate an attorney who has experience representing victims of domestic violence and sexual assault in their community. Many service providers keep a list of attorneys who will work for reduced fees.

Parties: This term refers to people involved in the case:

the person who starts the case, (usually the victim);

the person (s) who are named as involved in the case (usually the person alleged to be the abuser).

Person Eligible for Relief (PEFR):   Under Maryland law any of the following people can be given protection from domestic violence: the current or former spouse of the respondent (that is, the alleged abuser); a cohabitant of the respondent; a person related to the respondent by blood, marriage, or adoption; a parent of the respondent; a step-parent of the respondent; child or step-child of the respondent; victim who lives (or lived) with the respondent for at least ninety (90) days within the past year; or a vulnerable adult or individual who had a child with the respondent.

Petition for Contempt: Papers filed with court by either party in which one person alleges (or claims) that the opposing party has not followed with the terms of the Protective Order. After receiving the Petition, the Court will schedule a hearing to hear argument/testimony about the alleged violation of the protective order.

Petition for Protection: The request to the court in the protective order process. The Petition for Protection outlines why the Petitioner fears for her/his safety and indicates the type of relief s/he is asking the Court to order. After filing a Petition, the petitioner will immediately go before a Judge for a Temporary Protective Order hearing.

Petition to Modify: A request to the court that can be filed by either party when they want to change any part of the Protective Order. The Court will schedule a hearing to hear arguments/testimony about your reason for requesting a modification to the current Order.

Petitioner: The person requesting the court's help (typically, the alleged victim of abuse). The petitioner is not necessarily the same person as the person eligible for relief. The petitioner can also be any blood relative of a household member. (Family Law section 4-501).

POARP: Protective Order Advocacy and Representation Project: representing and acting as advocates for survivors of domestic violence whom are seeking protection from their abusers. This project is performed through a partnership of the House of Ruth and the Women's Law Center.

Prevention: Reduction of risk of occurrences, or delay of occurrences, of an adverse health, mental health, or other outcome. Prevention strategies can be characterized as universal, selective, or indicated (or respectively, primary, secondary, and tertiary) based on the level of risk associated with the groups or individuals for whom the intervention is intended.

Universal/Primary Prevention: Strategies applied to the general population with the purpose of preventing occurrences.

Selective/Secondary Prevention: Strategies targeting a particular population determined to be at-risk with the purpose of preventing occurrences.

Indicated/Tertiary Prevention: Strategies targeted to persons for whom adverse outcomes or problems have already occurred with the purpose of preventing reoccurrence.

Protective Factors: Characteristics, variables and/or conditions present in individuals or groups that enhance resiliency, increase resistance to risk, and fortify against the development of a disorder or adverse outcome. Examples would be constitutional factors like attractiveness or engaging personality, and bonding to family, school, and other social institutions.

Relief: "Relief" refers to the types of help that the judge or the District Court Commissioner are allowed by law order.

Respondent: The person against whom a petition is filed. In a domestic violence case this is the legal term used to refer to the person who is alleged to be the abuser.

Risk Factors: Characteristics, variables and/or conditions present in individuals or groups that increase the likelihood of that individual or group developing a disorder or adverse outcome. Since both the potency and clustering of risk and protection can vary over time and developmental periods, successful, developmentally appropriate prevention and interventions take this into account. Examples would be the availability of alcohol; unclear family rules, expectations, rewards; and permissive community laws and norms.

Service: Before a petitioner can have a Protection Order hearing, the respondent must be served (officially given) a copy of the petition by a law enforcement officer. If the respondent is not served, the Protective Order hearing will be rescheduled, typically the following week.

Sliding Scale: This term indicates that the fee you will be charged is based on the income you have available to you. Service providers will not charge victims and their families more than the families can afford. Most service providers will allow victims to have all services whether or not the victims are covered by insurance.

Temporary Protective Order (TPO): As a result of a hearing before a Judge, a special order is issued that provides protection from domestic violence. If the petitioner files for protection during the court's business hours, the TPO offers protection temporally until a Final Protective Order hearing can be scheduled and held:

If an-Interim Protective Order (IPO) was issued first, the TPO hearing is held within 24- 48 hours after the courts reopen.

Transitional Housing: Usually, furnished apartments that give residents the opportunity for independent living while they continue to access other resources (i.e. job training or family counseling).

Treatment: Treatment is a form of intervention that is typically long-term and characterized by an ongoing relationship with a particular type of service provider, most often a counselor, mental health clinician, or medical personnel. The goal of treatment is intended to provide long-term support and remediation of symptoms.

Use and Possession of a Vehicle: This term refers to the ability of the court to order that the petitioner can have temporary use and possession of a vehicle or house even though it is titled to both the petitioner and the respondent. To be given temporary use of the vehicle you must show that the vehicle is needed for employment and/or care of the minor child/children that you have with the respondent.

Vacate (An order to): A court order which requires the respondent to leave the home that the parties have shared. Abuse must have occurred while the parties were living together. The petitioner must also be listed on the deed or lease OR must have resided in the home for at least ninety (90) days in the past year.

Vulnerable Adult: Adults over the age of 18 who are unable to protect themselves, provide for their own daily needs, or get help when they are physically or emotionally abused. Such an individual may be vulnerable because of a physical or mental condition, as well as an increased physical weakness due to advanced age. MD Family § 14-101(q).

References For Glossary

Canada-Ukraine Gender Fund

http://www.genderfund.com.ua/glossary.htm

Source: Maryland Legal Assistance Network (MLAN) with the additional material from the materials," Domestic Violence Protective Orders Available 24/7" prepared by Dorothy Lennig-House of Ruth Legal Clinic.
http://www.peoples-law.org/domviol/glossary/glossary.htm

2003 National Center for Children Exposed to Violence (NCCEV)
Modification: April 14, 2003
http://www.nccev.org/resources/glossary_terms.html

Speak Truth to Power http://www.speaktruth.org/defend/glossary.html

BIBLIOGRAPHY

American Psychological Association. <u>Violence and the Family.</u> Washington, D.C. 1996

Carpenter, D. Lectures Howard University School of Divinity – History And Philosophy of Religious Education. Washington, DC 2005

Coker AL, Smith PH, McKeown RE, Melissa KJ. Frequency and correlates of intimate partner violence by type: physical, sexual, and psychological battering. American Journal of Public Health 2000;90(4):553–9.

Denny, D. <u>A Soldier Looks at Spiritual Warfare</u> Grand Rapids, MI: Chosen Books. 2004.

Felitti V, Anda R, Nordenberg D, Williamson D, Spitz A, Edwards V, et al. Relationship of childhood abuse and household dysfunction to many of the leading causes of death in adults. American Journal of Preventive Medicine 1998;14(4):245–58.

Gunthrie, S. Jr. <u>Christian Doctrine </u>Louisville, KY: Westminster John Knox Press (Revised Ed. 1994).

Figley, C. <u>The Compassion Fatigue Process, Self Care for the Practitioner,</u> Seminar Howard University Hospital, Washington, DC. 2005

BIBLIOGRAPHY

Fortune, M. Sexual Violence, The Unmentionable Sin
Cleveland, OH: The Pilgrim Press. 1983

Freire, P. Pedagogy of the Oppressed.
State & City: Continuum International Publishing Group; 30th
Anniversary Edition   (September 2000)

Garity, R. Mediation and Domestic Violence
Owego, NY: A New Hope Center.

Hammond, Frank & Ida. Pigs in the Parlor, The Practical Guide to
Deliverance

Kirkwood, MO: Impact Christian Books, Inc. 1973, 2004

Hodgson, P. Christian Faith A Brief Introduction
Louisville, KY: Westminster John Knox Press.2001.

King James Version Holy Bible

Koss M, Goodman L, Browne A, Fitzgerald L, Keita G, Russo N. No
Safe Haven   Male Violence Against Women at Home, At Work,
and In the Community. American Psychological Association,
Washington, DC 1994

Maryland Network Against Domestic Violence. "It Shouldn't Hurt to Go Home", Adapted from original booklet created by Idaho Coalition Against Sexual and Domestic Violence (Revised May 1999)

Maryland Network Against Domestic Violence. Standards for Domestic Violence Programs in Maryland Draft Procedures. 2004

McGrath, A. Christian Theology – An Introduction, 3rd Ed. Malden, MA: Blackwell Publishers Inc. 2001

McGrath, A. The Christian Theology Reader, 2nd Ed. Malden, MA: Blackwell Publishers Inc. 2001

Migliore, DL Faith Seeking Understanding – An Introduction to Christian Theology. Grand Rapids, MI: William B. Eerdmans Publishing Company. 1991

National Research Council. Understanding Violence Against Women. Washington (DC): National Academy Press; 1996. p. 74–80.

Poling, J. Understanding Male Violence Pastoral Care Issues Danvers, MA: Chalice Press.2003

Paulozzi LJ, Saltzman LA, Thompson MJ, Holmgreen P. Surveillance for homicide among intimate partners—United States, 1981–1998. CDC Surveillance Summaries 2001;50(SS-3):1–16.

BIBLIOGRAPHY

Robeson, Jerry & Carol <u>Strongman's His Name... What's His Game?</u>
Woodburn, OR: Shiloh Publishing House.1999

Roizen J. Issues in the epidemiology of alcohol and violence. In: Martin
SE, editor. Alcohol and Interpersonal Violence: Fostering multidis-
ciplinary perspectives. Bethesda (MD): National Institute on
Alcohol Abuse and Alcoholism; 1993. p. 3–36. NIAAA Research
Monograph No. 24.

Sanders, C. Lectures Howard University School of Divinity – Christian
Social Ethics. Washington, DC 2005

Schellenbach, C & Trickett,P <u>Violence Against Children in the Family</u>
<u>and the Community</u> Washington, D.C. American Psychological
Association. 1998

Straus MA, Gelles, RJ, editors. Physical Violence in American Families:
Risk factors and adaptations to violence in 8,145 families. New
Brunswick (NJ): Transaction Books; 1990.

Tjaden P, Thoennes N. Full Report of the Prevalence, Incidence, and
Consequences of Intimate Partner Violence Against Women:
Findings from the National Violence Against Women Survey.
Report for grant 93-IJ-CX-0012, funded by the National Institute of
Justice and the Centers for Disease Control and Prevention.
Washington (DC): NIJ; 2000.

Tjaden P, Thoennes N. Extent, Nature, and Consequences of Intimate Partner Violence: Findings from the National Violence Against Women Survey. Report for grant 93-IJ-CX-0012, funded by the National Institute of Justice and the Centers for Disease Control. Washington (DC): NIJ; 2000.

United Way of Massachusetts Bay. Inside Out, Tools to help faith-based organizations measure, learn, and grow   University of Maryland University College. Course Guide, BEHS454 – Family Violence (1st Ed). 1992

US Department of Justice. "Bureau of Justice Statistics 2002: At a Glance Walking In the Light –The Church Responds to Domestic Violence (New York Theological Seminary 1995)

Wicks R, Parsons R, Capps D, Clinical Handbook of Pastoral Counseling, Vol. 1 Paulist Press, Mahwah, NJ. 1985

Willis, A. T. Jr. MasterLife: The Disciple's Victory Nashville, TN: LifeWay Press. 1996

Wisner CL, Gilmer TP, Saltzman LE, Zink TM. Intimate partner violence against   women: do victims cost health plans more? Journal of Family Practice 1999;48(6):439–43.

Notes

1 Faith Seeking Understanding, p. 139

2 Westminster Dictionary, pp. 214

Resources

Prince George's County/Maryland Hotlines

The Family Crisis Center- 301-731-1203 or 1-866-382-7474 (24 hour hotline)
Provides a 24 hour domestic violence hotline, shelter, legal assistance, counseling and education

House of Ruth- 1-410-889-RUTH (24 hour hotline)

Sexual Assault Center- PG Hospital Center- 301-618-3154

Legal Forms Helpline-1-800-818-9888
The Helpline provides information on the use and completion of legal forms, and provides descriptions of court proceedings and some explanation of court instructions. Tuesday, Wednesday, and Friday 9 a.m. - 12:30 p.m. and Thursday 9 a.m. – 4 p.m.

Sexual Assault/Spouse Abuse Resource Center- 1(410) 836-8430
Provides a 24 hour domestic violence hotline, counseling, legal assistance and shelter.

CASA- (301) 739-8975
Provides a 24 hour domestic violence hotline, shelter, legal assistance, and job placement services. Washington County Only.

Nationwide Hotlines
Child Abuse
Child Help USA National Child Abuse Hotline: 800-4-A-CHILD (422-4453) or 800-2-A-CHILD (222-4453, TDD for hearing impaired)

•   Provides multilingual crisis intervention and professional counseling on child abuse. Gives referrals to local social service groups offering counseling on child abuse. Operates 24 hours, seven days a week.

Department of Social Services for public to access information:

- 800-345-KIDS: Provides information concerning children available for adoption and other children's programs
- 800-342-3009: Access to general information regarding Department programs and HEAP Hotline
- 800-732-5207: Day Care Complaint Line
- 800-342-3720: Child Abuse Hotline

National Child Abuse Hotline: 1-800-25-ABUSE

Crisis Intervention/Suicide
Covenant House Hotline: 800-999-9999

- Crisis line for youth, teens, and families. Gives callers locally based referrals throughout the United States. Provides help for youth and parents regarding drugs, abuse, homelessness, runaway children, and message relays. Operates 24 hours, seven days a week.

Domestic Violence
National Domestic Violence/Child Abuse/Sexual Abuse: 800-799-SAFE or 800-799-7233 or 800-787-3224 TDD or 800-942-6908 (Spanish Speaking)

- 24-hour-a-day hotline, Provides crisis intervention and counseling and referrals to local services and shelters for victims of partner or spousal abuse. English and Spanish speaking advocates are available 24 hours a day, 7 days a week. Staffed by trained volunteers who are ready to connect people with emergency help in their own communities, including emergency services and shelters. The staff can also provide information and referrals for a variety of non-emergency services, including counseling for adults and children, and assistance in reporting abuse. They have an extensive database of domestic violence treatment providers in all U.S. states and territories. Many staff members speak languages besides English, and they have 24-hour access to translators for approximately 150 languages. For the hearing impaired, there is a TDD number. This is a great resource for everyone- man, woman, and child- who is experiencing or has experienced domestic violence or abuse, or who suspects that someone they know is being abused.

Domestic Violence Hotline: 800-829-1122

Eating and Associated Disorders
National Association of Anorexia Nervosa & Associated Disorders (ANAD):
847-831-3438 (long distance)

National Mental Health Association: 800-969-6642 9 a.m. - 5 p.m. Mon-Fri
Information on mental health topics and referrals, access to an info specialist

Elder Abuse
Elder Abuse Hotline: 800-252-8966

Rape
Nationwide RAINN National Rape Crisis Hotline: 800-656-4673

Runaway/Exploited Children
Missing Children Network: 800-235-3535

The National Call Center for At-Risk Youth: (818) 710-1181

National Hotline for Missing and Exploited Children: 800-843-5678
Operates a hotline for reporting missing children and sightings of missing children. Offers assistance to law enforcement agents. Hours of operation are 7:30 a.m. - 11 p.m. EST

National Runaway Switchboard: 800-621-4000
Provides crisis intervention and travel assistance to runaways. Provides information and local referrals to adolescents and families. Gives referrals to shelters nationwide. Also relays messages to, or sets up conference calls with parents at the request of the child. Operates 24 hours, 7 days a week.

Child Find of America Hotline: 800-I-AM-LOST (426-5678)
Looks for missing and abducted children. Operators available 9 a.m. to 5 p.m. EST Monday- Friday. Voicemail on evenings and weekends with calls returned.

CONFIDENTIAL Runaway Hotline: 800-231-6946

Parent Abduction Hotline: 800-292-9688
Provides crisis mediation in parental abduction. Provides prevention information and referrals to local agencies. Operators available 9 a.m. to 5 p.m. EST Monday- Friday. Voicemail on evenings weekends with calls returned.

Youth

National Youth Crisis Hotline: 800-442-HOPE (4673)

•   Provides counseling and referrals to local drug treatment centers, shelters, and counseling services. Responds to youth dealing with pregnancy, molestation, suicide, and child abuse. Operates 24 hours, 7 days a week.